How Big Banks Fail and What to Do about It

How Big Banks Fail and What to Do about It

Darrell Duffie

PRINCETON UNIVERSITY PRESS
PRINCETON AND OXFORD

Copyright © 2011 by Princeton University Press

Published by Princeton University Press,
41 William Street, Princeton, New Jersey 08540

In the United Kingdom: Princeton University Press,
6 Oxford Street, Woodstock, Oxfordshire OX20 1TW

press.princeton.edu

Library of Congress Cataloging-in-Publication Data

Duffie, Darrell.
    How big banks fail and what to do about it / Darrell Duffie.
      p. cm.
    Includes bibliographical references and index.
    ISBN 978-0-691-14885-4 (alk. paper)
    1. Bank failures. 2. Bank failures—Prevention.
    3. Bank failures—United States. 4. Financial crises. I. Title.

HG1573.D84 2010
332.1—dc22   2010032251

British Library Cataloging-in-Publication Data is available

This book has been composed in LucidaBright using TₑX
Typeset by T&T Productions Ltd, London

Printed on acid-free paper. ∞
Printed in the United States of America

10 9 8 7 6 5 4 3 2

To Frankie

Contents

Figures and Tables

TABLES

Preface

AS WE COME OUT OF the financial crisis of 2007–2009, success in placing our financial system on a sounder footing depends on an understanding of how the largest and most connected banks, the major dealer banks, can make a sudden transition from weakness to failure. The dealer banks are at the center of the plumbing of the financial system. Among many other crucial activities, they intermediate over-the-counter markets for securities and derivatives. Although the financial crisis has passed, the dealer banks remain among the most serious points of instability in the financial system.

Once the solvency of a dealer bank is questioned, its relationships with its customers, equity investors, secured creditors, derivatives counterparties, and clearing bank can change suddenly. The incentives at play are similar to those of a depositor run at a commercial bank. That is, fear over the solvency of the bank leads to a rush by many to reduce their potential losses in the event that the bank fails: At first, the bank must signal its strength, giving up some of its slim stocks of remaining capital and cash, for to do otherwise would increase perceptions of weakness. Eventually, it is impossible for the bank to stem the tide of cash outflows. The bank then fails.

The key mechanisms of a dealer-bank failure, such as the collapses of Bear Stearns and Lehman Brothers in 2008, depend on special institutional and regulatory frameworks that influence the flight of short-term secured creditors, hedge-fund clients, derivatives counterparties, and most devastatingly, the loss of clearing and settlement services. Dealer banks, sometimes referred to as "large complex financial institutions" or as "too big to fail," are indeed of a size and complexity that sharply distinguish them from typical commercial banks. Even today, the failure of a dealer bank would pose a significant risk to the entire financial system and the wider economy.

Current regulatory approaches to mitigating bank failures do not adequately treat the special risks posed by dealer banks. Some of the required reforms are among those suggested in 2009 by the Basel Committee on Banking Supervision (2009) and in pending U.S. legislation, namely the Restoring American Financial Stability Bill. Additional needed reforms to regulations or market infrastructure still do not receive adequate attention. A January 2010 speech by Paul Tucker, Deputy Governor of the Bank of England, shows that some regulators are aware of the significant changes still required.[1]

In *How Big Banks Fail,* I describe the failure mechanics of dealer banks in clinical detail, as well as outline improvements in regulations and market infrastructure that are likely to reduce the risks of these failures and reduce the damage they cause to the wider financial system when they do fail.

I am grateful for impetus to this project from Andrei Shleifer and Jeremy Stein, for research assistance from Ross Darwin, Vojislav Sesum, Felipe Varas, and Zhipeng Zhang, and for helpful conversations with Joseph Abate, Viral Acharya, Tobias Adrian, J. A. Aitken, Yacov Amihud, Martin Bailey, Hugo Bänziger, John Berry, Robert Bliss, Michael Boskin, Lucinda Brickler, Jeremy Bulow, John Campbell, John Coates, John Cochrane, Andrew Crockett, Qiang Dai, Peter DeMarzo, Doug Diamond, Bill Dudley, Espen Eckbo, David Fanger, Alessio Farhadi, Peter Fisher, Mark Flannery, Ken French, John Goggins, Jacob Goldfield, Jason Granet, Ken Griffin, Joe Grundfest, Robert E. Hall, Dick Herring, Brad Hintz, Tom Jackson, Anil Kashyap, Matt King, Paul Klemperer, Alex Klipper, Bill Kroener, Eddie Lazear, Matt Leising, Paul Klemperer, Jean-Pierre Landau, Joe Langsam, Ada Li, Theo Lubke, David Mengle, Andrew Metrick, Rick Mishkin, Stewart Myers, Raghu Rajan, Eric Rosengen, Ken Scott, Manmohan Singh, Bob Shiller, Hyun Shin, David Scharfstein, Brendon Shvetz, Manmohan Singh, David Skeel, Matt Slaughter, Jeremy Stein, René Stulz, Kimberly Summe, Glen Taksler, John Taylor, Lauren Teigland-Hunt, Rick Thielke, Paul Tucker, Peter Wallison, Andrew White, Alex Wolf, Alex Yavorsky, Haoxiang Zhu, and Tatjana Zidulina. For their guidance, I also thank Ann Norman and Timothy Taylor from the *Journal of Economic Perspectives*, which published a shorter version of this work under the title "The Failure Mechanics of Dealer Banks," in February 2010.

I am also grateful to Linda Truilo for expert copyediting. Finally, I am grateful to Janie Chan, Seth Ditchik, Peter Dougherty, and Heath Renfroe of Princeton University Press.

Darrell Duffie
Stanford University, March, 2010

How Big Banks Fail and What to Do about It

CHAPTER ONE

Introduction

I BEGIN WITH A STORY of the failure of a bank that is a major dealer in securities and derivatives. Our dealer bank will be unable to stop the drain of cash caused by the departures of its short-term creditors, over-the-counter (OTC) derivatives counterparties, and client hedge funds. The most immediate examples are the 2008 failures of Bear Stearns and Lehman, but the failure mechanics at work could apply to any major dealer bank, once it is sufficiently weakened. There are further lessons to be learned from the major dealers such as Morgan Stanley that did not fail despite severe stresses on their liquidity shortly after the Lehman bankruptcy.

We pick up the story several months before the demise of a hypothetical dealer bank, which we shall call Beta Bank. Beta's capital position has just been severely weakened by losses. The cause need not be a general financial crisis, although that would further reduce Beta's chance of recovery. Once weakened, Beta takes actions that worsen its liquidity position in a rational gamble to signal its strength and protect its franchise value. Beta wishes to reduce the flight of its clients, creditors, and counterparties.

Beta's first move is to bail out some clients from the significant losses that they suffered through investments arranged by Beta. This is an attempt to maintain the value of Beta's reputation for serving its clients' interests. As time passes, and the cracks in Beta's finances become apparent to some market participants, Beta notices that some of its OTC derivatives counterparties have begun to lower their exposures to Beta. Their transactions slant more and more toward trades that drain cash away from Beta and toward these counterparties. Beta believes that it must continue to offer competitive terms on these trades, for to do otherwise would signal financial weakness, thereby exacerbating the flight. Other dealer banks are increasingly being asked to enter derivatives trades, called "novations," which have the effect of inserting the other dealers between Beta and its original derivatives counterparties, insulating those counterparties from Beta's default risk. As those dealers notice this trend, they begin to refuse novations that would expose them to Beta's default. As a result, the market gossip about Beta's weakness begins to circulate more rapidly.

Beta has been operating a significant prime-brokerage business, offering hedge funds such services as information technology, trade execution, accounting reports, and—more important to our story—a repository for the hedge funds' cash and securities. These hedge funds have heard the rumors and have been watching the market prices of Beta's equity and debt in order to gauge Beta's prospects. They begin to shift their cash and securities to better-capitalized prime brokers or, safer yet, to custodian banks. Beta's franchise value is thus rapidly eroding; its prospects for a merger rescue or for raising additional equity capital diminish accordingly. Potential providers of new equity capital question whether their capital infusions would do much more than improve the position of Beta's creditors. In the short run, a departure of prime-brokerage clients is also playing havoc with Beta's cash liquidity, because Beta has been financing its own business in part with the cash and securities left with it by these hedge funds. As they leave, Beta's cash flexibility declines to alarming levels.

Although Beta's short-term secured creditors hold Beta's securities as collateral against default losses, at this point they see no good reason to renew their loans to Beta. Potentially, they could get caught up in the administrative mess that would accompany Beta's default. Moreover, even though the amount of securities that they hold as collateral includes a "haircut"—a buffer for unexpected reductions in the market value of the collateral—there remains the risk that they could not sell the collateral at a high enough price to cover their loans. Most of these creditors fail to renew their loans to Beta. A large fraction of these short-term secured loans are in the form of repurchase agreements, or "repos." The majority of these have a term of one day. Thus, on short notice, Beta must find significant new financing, or conduct costly fire sales of its securities.

Beta's liquidity position is now grave. Beta's treasury department is scrambling to maintain positive cash balances in its clearing accounts. In the normal course of business, Beta's clearing bank would allow Beta and other dealers the flexibility of daylight overdrafts. A clearing bank routinely holds the dealer's securities in amounts sufficient to offset potential cash shortfalls. Today, however, Beta receives word that its clearing bank has exercised its right to stop processing Beta's cash transactions, given the exposure of the clearing bank to Beta's overall position. This is the last straw. Unable to execute its trades, Beta declares bankruptcy.

Beta Bank is a fictional composite. In what follows, my goal is to establish a factual foundation for the key elements of this story. In addition to providing institutional and conceptual frameworks, I will propose revisions to regulations and market infrastructure.

ECONOMIC PRINCIPLES

The basic economic principles at play in the failure of a large dealer bank are not so different from those of a garden-variety run on a typical retail bank, but the institutional mechanisms and the systemic destructiveness are rather different.

A conventional analysis of the stability of a bank, along the lines of Diamond and Dybvig (1983), conceptualizes the bank as an investor in illiquid loans. Financing the loans with short-term deposits makes sense if the bank is a superior intermediator between depositors, who are usually interested in short-term liquidity, and borrowers, who seek project financing. The equity owners of the bank benefit, to a point, from leverage. Occasionally, perhaps from an unexpected surge in the liquidity demands of depositors or from a shock to the ability of borrowers to repay their loans, depositors may become concerned over the bank's solvency. If the concern is sufficiently severe, the anticipation by depositors of a run is self-fulfilling.

The standard regulatory tools for treating the social costs of bank failures are the following: supervision and risk-based capital requirements, which reduce the chance of a solvency threatening loss of capital; deposit insurance, which reduces the incentives of individual depositors to trigger cash insolvency by racing each other for their deposits; and regulatory resolution mechanisms that give authorities the power to restructure a bank relatively efficiently. These regulatory tools not only mitigate the distress costs of a given bank and protect its creditors, but they also lower the knock-on risks to the rest of the financial system. We will consider some additional policy mechanisms that more specifically address the failure risks of large dealer banks.

Although I will simplify the discussion by treating large dealer banks as members of a distinct class, in practice they vary in many respects. They typically act as intermediaries in the markets for securities, repurchase agreements, securities lending, and over-the-counter derivatives. They conduct proprietary (speculative) trading in conjunction with these services. They are prime brokers to hedge funds and provide asset-management services to institutional and wealthy individual investors. As part of their asset-management businesses, some operate "internal hedge funds" and private equity partnerships, for which the bank acts effectively as a general partner with limited-partner clients. When internal hedge funds and other off-balance-sheet entities such as structured investment vehicles and money-market funds suffer heavy losses, the potential for a reduction in the dealer's reputation and franchise value gives the dealer bank an incentive to compensate investors voluntarily in these vehicles.

Dealer banks may have conventional commercial banking operations, including deposit taking as well as lending to corporations and consumers. They may also act as investment banks, which can involve managing and underwriting securities issuances and advising corporate clients on mergers and acquisitions. Investment banking sometimes includes "merchant banking" activities, such as buying and selling oil, forests, foodstuffs, metals, or other raw materials.

Large dealer banks typically operate under the corporate umbrella of holding companies. These are sometimes called "large complex financial institutions." Some of their activities are therefore outside of the scope of traditional bank-failure resolution mechanisms such as conservatorship or receivership.[1] New U.S. legislation, particularly the Restoring American Financial Stability Bill, extends the authority of the government to restructure large failing bank–holding companies and other systemically important financial institutions that were not already covered by traditional resolution mechanisms.

When the solvency of a dealer bank becomes uncertain, its various counterparties and customers have incentives to reduce their exposures to the bank, sometimes quickly and in a self-reinforcing cascade. Although their incentives to exit are similar to those of uninsured bank depositors, the mechanisms at play make the stability of a dealer bank worthy of additional policy analysis, especially considering the implications for systemic risk. Dealer banks have been viewed, with good reason, as "too big to fail." The destructiveness of the failure of Lehman Brothers in September 2008 is a case in point.

Although all large dealer banks now operate as regulated banks or within regulated bank–holding companies that have access to traditional and new sources of government or central-bank support, concerns remain over the systemic risk that some of these financial institutions pose to the economy. Although access to government support mitigates systemic risk associated with catastrophic failures, the common knowledge that too-big-to-fail financial institutions will receive support when they are sufficiently distressed—in order to limit disruptions to the economy—provides an additional incentive to large financial institutions to take inefficient risks, a well-understood moral hazard. The creditors of systemically important financial institutions may offer financing at terms that reflect the likelihood of a government bailout, thus further encouraging these financial institutions to increase leverage.

Among the institutional mechanisms of greatest interest here are those associated with short-term "repo" financing, OTC derivatives, off-balance-sheet activities, prime brokerage, and loss-of-cash settlement privileges at a dealer's clearing bank. Counterparty treatment at the failure of the dealer is a boundary condition that may accelerate a run once it begins.

As counterparties and others begin to exit their relationships with a distressed dealer bank, not only is the cash liquidity position of the bank threatened, but its franchise value also diminishes, sometimes precipitously. If the balance sheet or franchise value has significant associated uncertainty, potential providers of additional equity capital or debt financing, who might hope to profit by sharing in a reduction in distress losses, may hold back in light of adverse selection. They would be purchasing contingent claims whose prospects could be much more transparent to the seller (the bank) than to the investor. For example, during the 2008 financial crisis, when Wachovia was searching for a potential buyer of its business in order to avoid failure, a Wachovia official described the reluctance of Wells Fargo by saying[2] "They didn't understand our commercial loan book."

Another market imperfection, known as "debt overhang," further dampens the incentive of a weakened bank to raise new equity capital in order to lower its distress costs. Although large potential gains in the total enterprise value of a distressed bank could be achieved by the addition of equity capital, these gains would go mainly toward making creditors whole, which is not the objective of the current equity owners. Debt overhang is discussed in more detail in chapter 4.

In a normal distressed corporation, debt overhang and adverse selection can be treated by a bankruptcy reorganization, which typically eliminates the claims of equity owners and converts the claims of unsecured creditors to new equity. Attempts to restructure the debt of a large dealer bank, however, could trigger a rush for the exits by various clients, creditors, and derivatives counterparties. This may lead to a large fire sale, disrupting markets for assets and over-the-counter derivatives, with potentially destructive macroeconomic consequences. An automatic stay, which tends to preserve the enterprise value of a distressed non-financial company, can also limit the ability of a large dealer bank to manage its risk and liquidity. In any case, in many significant jurisdictions such as the United States, large classes of over-the-counter derivatives and repurchase agreements (short-term secured claims) are exempt from automatic stays, as explained by Krimminger (2006) and the International Swaps and Derivatives Association (2010). Jackson and Skeel (2010) analyze the efficacy of this exemption from automatic stays, from a legal viewpoint. The efficacy of this "safe harbor" for derivatives and repurchase agreements is a matter of significant debate.

Throughout this book I will pay special attention to reforms that go beyond those associated with conventional capital requirements, supervision, and deposit insurance. Among the additional mechanisms that might be used to address large-bank failure processes are central clearing counterparties for OTC derivatives, dedicated "utilities" for clearing tri-party repurchase agreements, forms of debt that convert to equity contingent on distress triggers, automatically triggered mandatory equity rights offerings, and regulations that require dealer banks to hold not only enough capital, but also enough liquidity, that is, enough uncommitted liquid assets to fill the hole left by sources of short-term financing that may disappear in a run.

In the next chapter, I review the typical structure and lines of business of a bank holding company whose subsidiaries intermediate over-the-counter markets for securities, repurchase agreements, and derivatives, among other investment activities that play a role in their failure mechanics. Chapter 3 then describes those failure mechanics. Chapter 4 reviews some impediments to the voluntary recapitalization of weakened financial institutions, and some contractual or regulatory mechanisms for automatic recapitalization when certain minimum capital or liquidity triggers are hit. Such automatic recapitalization mechanisms are among the main policy recommendations that are summarized in chapter 5. Other recommendations in this last chapter include minimum liquidity coverage ratios that incorporate the liquidity impact on a dealer bank of a potential flight by short-term secured creditors, derivatives counterparties, and prime-brokerage clients. I also recommend utility-style repo clearing banks. Another key recommendation, the central clearing of OTC derivatives, is described in more detail in the appendix.

CHAPTER TWO

What Is a Dealer Bank?

DEALER BANKS are financial institutions that intermediate the "backbone" markets for securities and over-the-counter (OTC) derivatives. These activities tend to be bundled with other wholesale financial market services, such as prime brokerage and underwriting. Because of their size and their central position in the plumbing of the financial system, the failure of a dealer bank could place significant stress on its counterparties and clients, and also on the prices of the assets or derivatives that it holds. The collapse of a major dealer bank also reduces the ability of the financial system to absorb further losses and to provide credit and liquidity to major market participants. Thus, the potential failure of a major dealer bank is a systemic risk.

Most if not all of the world's major dealer banks are among the financial institutions listed in table 2.1 that were invited to a meeting concerning over-the-counter derivatives at the New York Federal Reserve Bank on January 14, 2010. This list overlaps substantially with the list of primary dealers in U.S. government securities.[1] These firms typify large global financial groups that, in addition to their securities and derivatives businesses, may operate traditional commercial banks or have significant activities in investment banking, asset management, and prime brokerage.

The constellation of these various financial activities under the umbrella of one holding company presents a complex array of potential costs and benefits. The relevant research—for example, Boot, Milbourn, and Thakor (1999)—does not find a strong case for the net benefits of forming large diversified financial conglomerates of this type.[2] There are likely to be some economies of scope in information technology, marketing, financial innovation, and the diversification benefit of buffering many different sources of risk with a smaller number of pools of capital. Moreover, some of the risk-management failures among the large financial conglomerates, discovered during the crisis, probably reflect diseconomies of scope in risk

TABLE 2.1
Major dealers participating at the New York Federal Reserve Bank meeting on over-the-counter derivatives market infrastructure held on January 14, 2010.

BNP Paribas
Bank of America
Barclays Capital
Citigroup
Commerzbank AG
Credit Suisse
Deutsche Bank AG
Goldman, Sachs & Co.
HSBC Group
J. P. Morgan Chase
Morgan Stanley
The Royal Bank of Scotland Group
Société Générale
UBS AG
Wells Fargo

Source: New York Federal Reserve Bank.

management and corporate governance. It seems as though some senior executives and boards simply found it too difficult to comprehend or control some of the risk-taking activities inside their own firms.[3]

Proposals to limit the scope of risk-taking activities of large banks, such as that made by former Federal Reserve Chairman Paul Volcker,[4] are based on a desire to lower the probability of failure-threatening losses by precluding speculative activities beyond traditional loan provision and other client services. The "Volcker Rule" would also simplify the prudential supervision of large banks, because it would make them less complex. To be weighed against these benefits are the dangers of pushing a significant amount of risk-taking out of the regulated banking sector, and into the non-bank sector, where capital regulations and prudential supervision are likely to be less effective in limiting systemic risk. It may also be difficult to frame regulations that efficiently separate activities by which a bank speculates from those by which it takes risks in order to serve a client. For example, if a corporate client is best served by a bank loan that is tailored to reduce the client's currency risk or interest rate risk, a bank would normally lay off the currency or interest rate risk in a separate derivatives trade that could be difficult to identify as part of its client-service activities.

In the remainder of this chapter, I outline some of the key activities in which large dealer banks engage that can play a key role in their failure mechanics.

SECURITIES DEALING, UNDERWRITING, AND TRADING

Banks with securities businesses intermediate in the primary market between issuers and investors, and in the secondary market among investors. The driving concept is to buy low and sell high. Profits are earned in part though the provision of liquidity. In the primary market, the bank, sometimes acting as an underwriter, effectively buys equities or bonds from an issuer and then sells them over time to investors. In secondary markets, a dealer stands ready to have its bid prices hit by sellers and its ask prices lifted by buyers.

Dealers dominate the intermediation of over-the-counter securities markets, covering bonds issued by corporations, municipalities, many sovereign governments, and securitized credit products. OTC trades are privately negotiated. Trade between dealers in some derivatives and some securities, such as government bonds, is partially intermediated by interdealer brokers. Although public equities are easily traded on exchanges, dealers are also active in secondary markets for equities, acting as brokers or operators of "dark pools" (off-exchange order-crossing systems), securities custodians, securities lenders, or direct intermediaries in large-block trades.

Banks with dealer subsidiaries also engage in speculative investing, often called proprietary trading, aided in part by the ability to observe flows of capital into and out of certain classes of securities. Although legal "Chinese walls" may insulate proprietary traders from the information generated by securities dealing, there are nevertheless synergies between dealing and proprietary trading, based on common inventories of securities and cash, shared sources of external financing, and common human resources and infrastructure, such as information technology and trade-settlement "back office" systems.

Securities dealers also intermediate the market for repurchase agreements, or "repos." Putting aside some legal issues

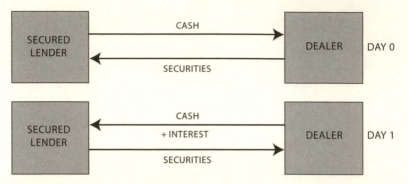

Figure 2.1. A repurchase agreement, or "repo."

that arise in bankruptcy, a repo is a short-term cash loan collateralized by securities. As figure 2.1 illustrates, one counterparty borrows cash from the other, and as collateral against performance on the loan, posts government bonds, corporate bonds, agency securities, or other debt securities such as collateralized debt obligations. Repos are frequently used for levered financing. For example, a hedge fund that specializes in fixed-income securities can finance the purchase of a large quantity of securities with a small amount of capital by placing purchased securities into repurchase agreements with a dealer, using the cash proceeds of the repo to purchase additional securities.

The majority of repurchase agreements are for short terms, typically overnight. In order to hold a security position over time, repurchase agreements are renewed with the same dealer or replaced by new repos with other dealers. The performance risk on a repo is typically mitigated by a "haircut" that reflects the risk or liquidity of the securities. For instance, a haircut of 10 percent allows a cash loan of $90 million to be obtained by posting securities with a market value of $100 million.

In order to settle their own repo and securities trades, dealers typically maintain clearing accounts with other major banks. J. P. Morgan Chase and the Bank of New York Mellon handle most dealer clearing. Access to clearing services is crucial to a dealer's daily operations. In the event that a dealer's clearing bank denies these services—for example, over credit concerns—the dealer would be unable to meet its daily obligations. It would fail almost instantly.

Repurchase agreements are frequently "tri-party" in nature. In 2007, according to Geithner (2008), tri-party repos involving primary dealers totaled approximately $2.5 trillion per day. As illustrated in figure 2.2, the third party is usually a clearing bank that holds the collateral and is responsible for returning the cash to the creditor. This arrangement is designed to facilitate trade and safe custody of the collateral. In theory, the clearing bank is merely an agent of the two repo counterparties. In practice, however, current tri-party repo practices also expose clearing banks to the default of the dealer banks, as we shall explain in chapter 3. The same two clearing banks, J. P. Morgan Chase and the Bank of New York Mellon, are dominant in tri-party repos. Some tri-party repos, particularly in Europe, are arranged through specialized repo clearing services, Clearstream and Euroclear. In the United States, the Fixed Income Clearing Corporation handled the clearing of approximately $1 trillion a day of U.S. Treasury repurchase agreements in 2008, according to its parent, the Depository Trust and Clearing Corporation.

A dealer is not simply a broker that matches buyers and sellers. Because the ultimate buyers and sellers do not approach the dealer simultaneously, and because their trades do not precisely offset each other, the dealer acts as a buyer and as a seller on its own account. Securities dealing is therefore risky. Long-run success depends not only on skill but also on access to a pool of capital that is able to absorb significant losses. Dealing also requires sufficient liquidity to handle large fluctuations in cash flows.

OVER-THE-COUNTER DERIVATIVES

Derivatives are contracts that transfer financial risk from one investor to another. For example, a call option gives an investor the right to buy an asset in the future at a pre-arranged price. Derivatives are traded on exchanges and over the counter (OTC). For most OTC derivatives trades, one of the two counterparties is a dealer. A dealer usually lays off much of the net risk of the derivatives positions requested by counterparties by entering new derivatives contracts with other counterparties, who are often other dealers. This is sometimes called a "matched book" dealer operation.

Figure 2.2. A tri-party repurchase agreement, by which a money-market fund lends cash to a dealer.

As in their securities businesses, dealer banks also conduct proprietary trading in OTC derivatives markets. Again, the basic idea is to buy low and sell high, on average, over many positions.

The notional amount of an OTC derivative contract is typically measured as the market value—or, in the case of debt-based derivatives, the face value—of the asset whose risk is transferred by the derivative. For example, a call option to buy 1 million shares of an equity whose price is $50 per share represents a notional position of $50 million dollars. A credit default swap has a notional size of $100 million if it offers default protection on $100 million principal of debt of the named borrower.

Currently, the total gross notional amount of OTC derivatives outstanding is roughly $600 trillion dollars, according to the Bank of International Settlements. (The gross notional amount of exchange-traded derivatives is roughly $400 trillion.) The majority of OTC derivatives are interest rate swaps, which are commitments to make periodic exchanges of one interest rate, such as the London Interbank Offering Rate (LIBOR), for another, such as a fixed rate on a given notional principal, until a stipulated maturity date. For example, a corporation may find that investors in its debt are more receptive to floating-rate notes than to fixed-rate notes, whereas the issuing corporation may prefer a fixed rate of interest expense, for example, because equity-market investors might otherwise bid down its shares if they are not confident of the sources of reported earnings fluctuations. The corporation may then issue floating-rate debt and also enter an interest rate swap, by which it makes coupon payments at a fixed rate and receives floating-rate payments.

The largest OTC derivatives dealer by volume is J. P. Morgan Chase & Company, with a total notional position recently measured at $79 trillion, according to data reported to the Office of the Comptroller of the Currency (2009). Bank of America Corporation, Goldman Sachs, Morgan Stanley, and Citigroup come next in terms of their notional holdings of derivatives, with $75 trillion, $50 trillion, $42 trillion, and $35 trillion, respectively.

As opposed to assets held in positive net supply, such as equities, the net total supply of any type of derivative is zero. Thus, the net total market value of all derivatives contracts is zero, as a mere accounting identity. For example, the call option in our simple example may have a substantial market value to the buyer, say $10 million. The seller in that case has a market value that is negative by the same amount, $10 million dollars. As contingencies are realized over time, derivatives transfer wealth from counterparty to counterparty, but do not directly add to or subtract from the total stock of wealth. Indirectly, however, derivatives can provide substantial benefits by transferring risk from those least prepared to bear it to those most prepared to bear it. Derivatives can also cause substantial distress costs. For instance, counterparties incurring large losses on derivatives contracts may be forced to incur frictional bankruptcy costs, and their failures to perform on their derivatives contracts may lead to large distress costs for their counterparties.

A useful gauge of counterparty risk in the OTC derivatives market is the amount of exposure to default presented by the failure of counterparties to perform their contractual obligations. In our simple option example, the current exposure of the buyer to the seller is the $10 million market value of the option, unless the seller has provided collateral against its obligation. If the seller provides $8 million in collateral, the exposure is reduced to $2 million.

Normally, the various OTC derivatives trades between a given pair of counterparties are legally combined under a "master swap agreement" between those two counterparties. The master swap agreements signed by dealers generally conform to standards set by the International Swaps and Derivatives Association (ISDA). Credit support annexes of these master swap agreements govern collateral requirements as well as the obligations of the two counterparties in the event that one of them cannot perform. In many cases, a counterparty to a dealer is required to post an "independent amount" of collateral with the dealer, which remains with the dealer for the life of the position.[5] In addition, as the market values of the derivatives contracts between any two counterparties fluctuate, the collateral required is recalculated, normally on a daily basis, according to terms stated in the credit support annex of their master swap agreement.

One of the key features of master swap agreements is the netting of exposures and of collateral requirements across different derivatives positions. For example, suppose that the owner of the call option that is worth 10 million dollars in our previous example is a dealer that also holds an oil forward contract with the same counterparty, whose market value to the dealer is − $4 million. In this case, the net exposure of the dealer to its counterparty is 10 − 4 = 6 million dollars, before collateral is considered. Netting lowers default exposure and lowers collateral requirements. As the financial crisis that began in 2007 deepened, the range of acceptable forms of collateral taken by dealers from their OTC derivatives counterparties was narrowed, leaving over 80 percent of collateral in the form of cash during 2008, according to a survey conducted by the International Swaps and Derivatives Association (2009). The total amount of collateral demanded also nearly doubled in 2008, from about $2 trillion in 2007 to about $4 trillion in 2008.

Table 2.2 shows the total gross exposures of major dealers in OTC derivatives of various types, as estimated from dealer surveys by the Bank for International Settlements (2009a), before considering netting and collateral. The table also shows a substantial reduction in exposure through netting. Despite the amount of concern that has been raised over counterparty default exposures on credit default swaps, which are in essence insurance against the default of a named borrower, this source of counterparty risk is small in comparison to that associated with interest rate swaps. Although interest rate swaps have market values that are less volatile than those of credit default swaps, the notional amount of interest rate swaps is over fifteen times that of credit default swaps, overwhelming the effect of volatility differences in terms of total counterparty credit exposures.

TABLE 2.2
Exposures of dealers in OTC derivatives markets as of June 2009. Net exposures do not include non-U.S. credit default swaps.

Asset class	Exposure ($ billions)
Credit default swap	2,987
Interest rate	15,478
Equity linked	879
Foreign exchange	2,470
Commodity	689
Unallocated	2,868
Total	25,372
Total after netting	3,744

Source: BIS, November, 2009.

While it is likely that the market values of credit default swaps would become even more volatile during a sudden financial crisis, the fact that dealer banks have relatively balanced short and long positions in credit default swaps partially insulates them from counterparty risk in such a scenario.

At least one of the two counterparties in most OTC derivatives trades is a dealer. It would be uncommon, for example, for a hedge fund to trade directly with, say, an insurance company. Instead, the hedge fund and the insurance company would normally trade with dealers. Dealers themselves frequently trade with other dealers. Further, when offsetting a prior OTC derivatives position, it is common for market participants to avoid negotiating the cancellation of the original derivatives contract. Instead, a new derivatives contract that offsets the bulk of the risk of the original position is frequently arranged with the same or another dealer. As a result, dealers accumulate large OTC derivatives exposures, often with other dealers.

Dealers are especially likely to be counterparties to other dealers in the case of a credit default swap (CDS). When a hedge fund decides to reduce a CDS position, a typical step in executing this offset is to have its original CDS position "novated" to another dealer, which then stands between the hedge fund and the original dealer by entering new back-to-back CDS positions with each, as illustrated in figure 2.3.

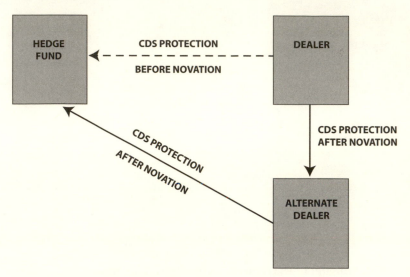

Figure 2.3.   Novation of a credit default swap.

In this fashion, dealer-to-dealer CDS positions grew rapidly in the years leading up to the financial crisis. Data provided by the Depository Trust and Clearing Corporation (DTCC) in January 2010 reveals that of the current aggregate notional amount of about $25.5 trillion in credit default swaps whose terms are collected by DTCC's DerivServ Trade Information Warehouse, over $20 trillion are in the form of dealer-to-dealer positions.[6] Since mid-2008, when the total notional size of the CDS market stood at over $60 trillion, the total amount of credit default swaps outstanding has been reduced dramatically by "compression trades," by which redundant or nearly redundant positions among dealers are effectively canceled.[7] Significant further reductions in counterparty exposures have also been obtained through clearing.

Prime Brokerage and Asset Management

Some large dealer banks are active as prime brokers to hedge funds and other large investors. In some cases, acting through broker-dealer subsidiaries, they provide these clients a range of services, including custody of securities, clearing, cash management services, securities lending, financing, and reporting (which may include risk measurement, tax accounting, and various other accounting services). A dealer may frequently serve as a derivatives counterparty to its prime-brokerage clients. A dealer often generates additional revenue by lending securities that are placed with it by prime-brokerage clients. As of the end of 2007, according to data from Lipper, the majority of prime-brokerage services were provided by just three firms, Morgan Stanley, Goldman Sachs, and Bear Stearns, whose prime-brokerage business was absorbed by J. P. Morgan when it acquired Bear Stearns in March 2008.[8]

Dealer banks often have large asset-management divisions that cater to the investment needs of institutional and wealthy individual clients. The services provided include custody of securities, cash management, brokerage, and investment in alternative asset-management vehicles, such as hedge funds and private-equity partnerships, which are typically managed by the same bank. Such an "internal hedge fund" may offer contractual terms similar to those of external stand-alone hedge funds, and in addition can wrap the limited partner's position within the scope of general asset-management services. At the end of 2009, the world's largest manager of hedge funds was J. P. Morgan Chase, with a total of $53.5 billion in hedge fund assets under management, according to Williamson (2010).

In addition to the benefit of "one-stop shopping," a limited partner in an internal hedge fund or private equity partnership may perceive that a large bank is more stable than a stand-alone hedge fund, and that the bank might voluntarily support an internal hedge fund financially at a time of need. For example, near the end of June 2007, Bear Stearns offered to lend $3.2 billion to one of its failing internal hedge funds, the High-Grade Structured Credit Fund.[9] In August of 2007, at a time of extreme market stress and losses to some of its internal hedge funds, Goldman Sachs injected[10] a significant amount of capital into one of them, the Global Equity Opportunities Fund. In February 2008, Citigroup provided $500 million in funding to an internal hedge fund known as Falcon.[11]

Off-Balance-Sheet Financing

In addition to financing asset purchases through traditional bond issuance, commercial paper, and repurchase agreements, among other liabilities, some large dealer banks have made extensive use of "off-balance-sheet" financing. For example, a bank can originate or purchase residential mortgages and other loans that are financed by selling them to a special purpose financial corporation or trust that it has set up expressly to fulfill this function as a purchaser of loans. Such a special purpose entity (SPE) pays its sponsoring bank for the assets with the proceeds of debt that it issues to third-party investors. The principal and interest payments of the SPE's debt are paid from the cash flows that, hopefully, it will receive from the assets that it has purchased from the sponsoring bank.

Because an SPE's debt obligations are normally contractually remote from the activities of the sponsoring bank, under certain conditions banks have not been required to treat the SPE's assets and debt obligations as though their own, for purposes of accounting and of regulatory minimum capital requirements. In this sense, an SPE is "off balance sheet." Off-balance-sheet financing has therefore allowed some large banks to operate much larger loan purchase and origination businesses, with a given amount of bank capital, than would have been possible had they held the associated assets on their own balance sheets. For example, in June 2008, Citigroup reported over $800 billion in off-balance-sheet assets held in such "qualified special purpose entities."

A form of special-purpose off-balance-sheet entity that was popular until the financial crisis is the structured investment vehicle (SIV), which finances residential mortgages and other loans with short-term debt sold to investors such as money-market funds. In 2007 and 2008, when home prices fell dramatically in the United States and subprime residential mortgage defaults rose, the solvency of many SIVs was threatened. The SIVs were in some cases unable to make their debt payments, especially as some short-term creditors to these funds recognized the solvency concerns and failed to renew their loans to SIVs. Some large dealer banks bailed out investors in some of the SIVs that they had set up. For example, in late 2007, HSBC voluntarily committed about $35 billion to bring the assets of its off-balance-sheet SIVs onto its balance sheet.[12] Citigroup followed in December 2007 by bringing $49 billion in SIV assets and liabilities onto its own balance sheet.[13]

As with support provided to distressed internal hedge funds, the equity owners and managers of these banks may have rationally perceived that the option of providing no recourse to their effective clients would have resulted in a loss of market value, through a reduction in reputation and market share, that exceeded the cost of the recourse actually taken. This amounts to "asset substitution," in the sense of Jensen and Meckling (1976), that is, a conscious increase in the risk of the bank's balance sheet, leading to an effective transfer of value from the bank's unsecured creditors to its equity holders. Some of these banks, had they been able to foresee the extent of their later losses during the financial crisis, might have preferred to allow their clients to fend for themselves.

CHAPTER THREE

Failure Mechanisms

THE RELATIONSHIPS BETWEEN A DEALER BANK and its derivatives counterparties, potential debt and equity investors, clearing bank, and clients can change rapidly if the solvency of the dealer bank is threatened. A dealer's liquidity can suddenly disappear, as illustrated in figure 3.1, which shows how quickly Bear Stearns's cash resources were depleted once its solvency came into question in March 2008. As explained in chapter 1, the concepts at play are not so different from those involved in a depositor run.

In this chapter, we describe the main processes by which a run on a dealer can occur, through OTC derivatives, repo, prime brokerage, and clearing.

REACTIONS BY OTC DERIVATIVES COUNTERPARTIES

At the perception of a potential solvency crisis of a dealer bank, an OTC derivatives counterparty to that bank would look for opportunities to reduce its exposure.

Initially, a counterparty could reduce its exposure by borrowing from the dealer, or by drawing on prior lines of credit with that dealer, or by entering new derivatives contracts with the dealer that would offset some of the exposure. A counterparty could also ask to have options that are in the money to be restruck at the money, so as to harvest some cash from the option position and thereby reduce exposure to the dealer. A counterparty to the dealer could also reduce its exposure to the weak dealer through novation to another dealer.[1] For instance, a hedge fund that had purchased protection from a dealer on a named borrower, using a credit default swap (CDS) contract, could contact a different dealer and ask that dealer for a novation, insulating the hedge fund from the default of the original dealer, as illustrated in figure 2.3. All of these actions reduce the dealer's cash position.

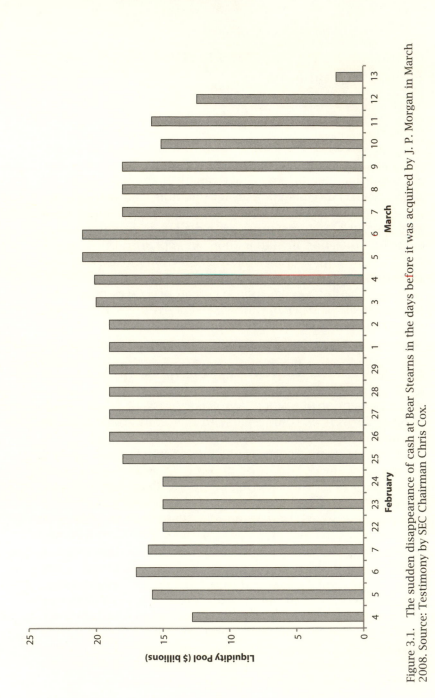

Figure 3.1. The sudden disappearance of cash at Bear Stearns in the days before it was acquired by J. P. Morgan in March 2008. Source: Testimony by SEC Chairman Chris Cox.

When Bear Stearns's solvency and liquidity were threatened in early March 2008, some of Bear Stearns's counterparties asked other dealers for novations, by which those dealers would effectively absorb the risk of a failure by Bear Stearns. Kelly (2008) reported that "[h]edge funds flooded Credit Suisse Group's brokerage unit with requests to take over trades opposite Bear Stearns. In a blast email sent out that afternoon, Credit Suisse stock and bond traders were told that all such novation requests involving Bear Stearns and any other 'exceptions' to normal business required the approval of credit-risk managers." Burroughs (2008) further reported: "That same day Bear executives noticed a worrisome development whose potential significance they would not appreciate for weeks. It involved an avalanche of what are called 'novation' requests. When a firm wants to rid itself of a contract that carries credit risk with another firm, in this case Bear Stearns, it can either sell the contract back to Bear or, in a novation request, to a third firm for a fee. By Tuesday afternoon, three big Wall Street companies—Goldman Sachs, Credit Suisse, and Deutsche Bank—were experiencing a torrent of novation requests for Bear instruments." Although dealers routinely grant such novations, in this case other dealers naturally began to refuse these Bear Stearns novations. This in turn is likely to have spread alarm over Bear Stearns's difficulties. Cohan (2009:27) writes of Goldman Sachs's refusal on March 11, 2008, to accept a novation of a credit default swap position between Hayman Capital's Subprime Credit Strategies Fund and Bear Stearns. Gary Cohn, copresident of Goldman Sachs, is quoted as telling the senior leadership of Bear Stearns, "If we start taking novations, people pull their business, they pull their collateral, you're out of business." Cohan also describes Goldman's offer the next morning to accept the novation.

As for Lehman, Valukas (2010:4:1236–38) writes that "as a result of Lehman's rapidly declining stock price, and negative market reactions to Lehman's earnings preannouncement and changes in upper-management, Citi experienced a three-fold increase in novation requests on June 12 [2010] for a total of approximately 26 novation requests to trade out of Lehman that week.... Citibank Global Financial Institutions Risk Management Risk Officer Thomas Fontana, in an internal June 12 Citi e-mail exchange, stated: 'Fuld oust[ed the] CFO and COO.... We have cut back clearing lines in Asia.... This is bad news. Market is saying Lehman can not make it alone. Loss of confidence here is huge at the moment. We are seeing novations and are passing on them!'"

Beyond heightening the concerns of investors, a rash of novations could place the original dealer's cash position under additional stress, because novations could be accompanied by removal of the independent amount of cash collateral that had been placed in the hands of the dealer by its novating counterparties.[2]

In the United States, Rules 15c3-2 and 15c3-3 of the Securities and Exchange Act of 1934 require broker-dealers to segregate "fully paid securities" and limit a broker-dealer's use of "free credit balances." These rules do not, however, apply to collateral held by the broker-dealer affiliates that typically hold the cash posted by derivatives counterparties as collateral.[3] The cash collateral that derivatives counterparties post with a dealer is not typically segregated from the dealer's own cash, and is therefore a useful source of liquidity to the dealer.[4] Although the standard International Swaps and Derivatives Association (ISDA) credit support annex signed by dealers stipulates that a bankrupt dealer must return any cash collateral owed to its counterparties, the dealer may simply refuse to do so, as Lehman Brothers did in some cases. If that occurs, the counterparty is left with a senior unsecured claim against the dealer's bankruptcy estate for the missing collateral. Recovery on that claim can be late and incomplete.[5] Faced with this potential loss, a counterparty to a weakening dealer would have an incentive to exit quickly its derivatives positions and retrieve its collateral.

The weakness of a dealer can also be exacerbated if its derivatives counterparties attempt to reduce their exposures to that dealer by entering new trades that cause that dealer to pay out cash. For example, suppose that a dealer with liquidity problems is asked for bid and ask quotations on an OTC option. If the bid price is accepted, the dealer would be required to settle with a cash payment to the counterparty. In light of its liquidity problems, the dealer could refuse to provide two-sided market quotations, or could provide obviously unattractive quotes, but this would signal its weakness to the market. As a consequence, in the initial stages of solvency concerns, a dealer that believes there is a reasonable chance of surviving a crisis would generally wish to signal its strength by continuing to make two-sided market quotations, despite the associated drain of cash to those counterparties who are attempting to reduce their exposures to the dealer.

The credit annexes of OTC derivatives master swap agreements call for the posting of additional collateral by a counterparty whose credit rating is downgraded below a stipulated level. A typical threshold for large dealers is a bond rating of A2 by Moodys or A by Standard and Poors.[6] For example, in its 10K filing with the Securities and Exchange Commission dated January 1, 2009, on page 82, Morgan Stanley disclosed that "[i]n connection with certain OTC trading agreements and certain other agreements associated with the Institutional Securities business segment, the Company may be required to provide additional collateral to certain counterparties in the event of a credit ratings downgrade. As of November 30, 2008, the amount of additional collateral that could be called by counterparties under the terms of collateral agreements in the event of a one-notch downgrade of the Company's long-term credit rating was approximately $498.3 million. An additional amount of approximately $1,456.2 million could be called in the event of a two-notch downgrade." The collateral-on-downgrade triggers of the master swap agreements of AIG Financial Products (not a dealer bank) were the most proximate cause of the need by AIG for a massive U.S. government bailout.

Master swap agreements also include terms for the early termination of derivatives in a selection of contingencies, including the default of one of the counterparties, which typically results in a termination settlement of the derivatives portfolio at what amounts to the replacement cost for the non-defaulting counterparty. For this, third-party prices, or terms for new derivatives with other counterparties, or model-based price estimates, would be obtained for the terminated derivatives positions. The actual procedures to be followed can be complicated, as appears to be case in the Lehman bankruptcy.[7]

The replacement of derivatives positions may represent a large new liability to a defaulting dealer, above and beyond the net market value of its positions at "mid-market" pricing, that is, at the mid-point between bid and ask quotations, which is the basis for the normal mark-to-market accounting of derivatives. For example, the holding company of Bank of America has in aggregate an OTC derivatives portfolio with a notional size of approximately $75 trillion, according to Office of the Comptroller of the Currency (OCC) data as of this writing.[8] If the average effective termination settlement liability associated with replacing counterparty positions, above and beyond mid-market valuations, is, for example, 0.1% of the notional position, then the effective new liability would be about $75 billion. Furthermore, because most OTC derivatives are executory contracts that are exempt from automatic bankruptcy stays, the termination settlement of OTC derivatives can proceed immediately, giving derivatives counterparties some effective priority over unsecured creditors whose claims are stayed by the bankruptcy process, such as unsecured bond claimants. The senior unsecured creditors of a major derivatives dealer would therefore view the OTC derivatives book of a dealer as a major incentive to exit their creditor positions, if possible, in the face of any concerns over the dealer's solvency. This could in turn accelerate the dealer's failure.

A rush by OTC derivatives counterparties to exit their positions with a weak or failed dealer could be disruptive to derivatives markets and to other financial markets and institutions.[9] This was the case at the default of Lehman Brothers in September 2008, despite the emergency attempts of other dealers to coordinate the replacement of their OTC derivatives positions with Lehman.[10]

The termination settlement of OTC derivatives portfolios could also be triggered by attempts to resolve a failing financial institution through an out-of-court restructuring. Consider, for example, the resolution of a distressed bank into a good bank and a bad bank, along the lines of the Swedish resolution of Nordbank, as described by Macey (1999). Suppose that the performing assets of a distressed dealer bank are to be transferred to a new "good bank," whose equity would be given to the unsecured creditors of the original bank, which is a resolution approach proposed by Bulow and Klemperer (2009). Even if the bank's creditors were to agree to such a restructuring outside of a bankruptcy or conservatorship, thereby avoiding the default termination settlement provisions of master swap agreements, the typical master swap agreement also calls for termination settlement in the event that a counterparty transfers the bulk of its assets to another entity in a manner that leaves the counterparty in a materially weaker condition.[11]

For OTC derivatives that are "cleared," that is, novated to a central clearing counterparty who stands between the original counterparties,[12] the counterparties to the dealer are insulated from the default of the dealer, assuming of course the performance of the central clearing counterparty. Although the dealer itself is subject to its obligations under any cleared derivatives, cleared derivatives should play little or no role in the incentives of counterparties to the dealer to rush for the exits, except perhaps for the incentives of a central clearing counterparty itself to reduce its exposure to the dealer.[13] Further, the incentive of unsecured lenders to a dealer bank to run in the face of the dealer's distress is lowered to the extent that the dealer's OTC derivatives have been cleared. Central clearing also mitigates the systemic risk associated with knock-on effects to the counterparties of a failing dealer that are themselves important financial institutions. Central clearing counterparties can handle only derivatives with relatively standard terms, however, and therefore would not have been in a position to mitigate the counterparty risks associated with the infamous AIG FP credit derivatives, which were highly customized.

In chapter 5, we return to consider the stabilizing role of central clearing counterparties in more detail. The appendix provides an overview of the operation and risk management of central clearing counterparties, including the treatment of a failing clearing member's positions.

THE FLIGHT OF SHORT-TERM CREDITORS

Large dealers tend to finance significant fractions of their assets with short-term repurchase agreements. The counterparties of these repos are often money-market funds, securities lenders, and other dealers. Repos with a term of one day, which are called "overnight repos," are common, as they offer maximal flexibility and, normally, the lowest market financing rates available. For example, from New York Federal Reserve Bank data on Financing by U.S. Government Securities Dealers,[14] of the total amount of dealer financing of treasuries, agency securities, mortgages, and corporate bonds, approximately 70% was financed overnight.

Under normal pre-crisis market conditions, a dealer bank might have been able to finance most of its holdings of agency securities, treasuries, corporate bonds, mortgages, and collateralized debt obligations by daily renewal of overnight repos with an average haircut of under 2%, thus allowing an effective leverage ratio of at least 50. The dealer could therefore hold these assets on its balance sheet with little capital. Before their failures, Bear Stearns and Lehman had gross (asset-to-capital) leverage ratios of over 30, with significant dependence on short-term repo financing.[15] By amalgamating on-balance-sheet accounting data with information from 10Q footnotes, King (2008) estimates that in the first half of 2008, about 42% of the financial instruments of broker-dealers were financed through repo or repo-equivalent transactions, as shown in table 3.1. For Bear Stearns, this fraction was 55%. At the end of 2007, the total dealer fraction was 48%, according to King's estimates.

Although the repo creditors providing cash to a dealer bank have recourse to the collateralizing assets, often with a haircut that protects them to some degree from fluctuations in the market value of the collateral, they may have little or no incentive to renew repos in the face of concerns over the dealer bank's solvency.[16]

In the event that the dealer counterparty fails to return their cash, the repo creditors would have an incentive, or could be legally required,[17] to sell the collateral immediately, could discover a shortfall in the cash proceeds of the collateral sale, and could potentially face litigation over allegations of improper disposal of the assets. The repo creditors can avoid these threats, and other unforeseen difficulties, simply by reinvesting their cash in new repos with other counterparties.

If a dealer bank's repo creditors fail to renew their positions en masse, the ability of the dealer to raise sufficient cash by other means on short notice is doubtful, absent emergency support from a government or central bank. Tucker (2009) has emphasized the importance of broad and flexible lender-of-last-

TABLE 3.1
Quarter-end financing of broker-dealer financial instruments before the failures of Bear Stearns and Lehman ($ billions).

	May-08 Morgan Stanley	May-08 Goldman Sachs	May-08 Lehman	June-08 Merrill Lynch	Feb-08 Bear Stearns	2nd Qtr Total
Financial instruments owned	390	411	269	289	141	1,501
pledged (and can be repledged)	140	37	43	27	23	271
pledged (and cannot be repledged)	54	121	80	53	54	362
not pledged at all	196	253	146	208	64	868
Fraction pledged	50%	39%	46%	28%	55%	42%

Source: King (2008).

resort financing. Aside from the direct risks posed to the creditors and the counterparties of a dealer bank that is suddenly unable to finance itself with repurchase agreements, there is the potential for a large asset fire sale that could have destructive impacts on other market participants through adverse marks to market on their own repo collateral. The proceeds of an asset fire sale might be insufficient to meet cash demands, especially if the solvency concerns were prompted by declines in the market values of the collateral assets themselves. Even if the dealer bank could quickly sell enough assets to meet its immediate cash needs, the fire sale could lead other market participants to make fatal inferences about the weakened condition of the dealer.

A dealer bank's financing problems could be exacerbated during a general financial crisis, when the declining transparency of some forms of repo collateral, or increases in the volatility of collateral valuations, could prompt dramatic increases in repo haircuts, which in turn could lead to fire sales, price declines, and further increases in haircuts, an adverse feedback cycle modeled by Geanakoplos (2003) and by Brunnermeier and Pedersen (2008). During the autumn of 2008, haircuts on investment-grade corporate bonds rose to as much as 20%, while repo financing of many forms of collateralized debt obligations and speculatively rated corporate bonds became essentially impossible.[18] Abate (2009) reported that corporate bond repo transactions (which include non-agency mortgage backed securities) fell approximately 60% between March 2008 and March 2009.

Table 3.2 shows the results of a survey of repo haircuts conducted by the Committee on the Global Financial System (2010). The table shows the extent to which haircuts increased between June 2007 (before the financial crisis) and June 2009 (after the most severe portion of the crisis). The table also shows that haircuts are often larger for less creditworthy counterparties.

Facing a dealer whose resources appear to be threatened, counterparties could attempt to raise haircuts specifically to that dealer, or reduce the range of acceptable collateral from that dealer, or dispute the pricing of the dealer's collateral. For instance, Cohan (2009) reports on the increasing set of Bear Stearns's normal repo counterparties who, during the week leading up to the failure of Bear Stearns, told the company that they would not be renewing their repo financing to it, or were applying more onerous haircuts and disputing repo collateral valuations.

If concerns over the creditworthiness of a dealer do come to light, the clearing bank that handles its tri-party repos, as well as the repo counterparties providing cash to the dealer, are likely to consider the implications of a failure by the dealer to return the cash due on its repos. If that were to happen, the cash-providing counterparty might be given the securities posted by the dealer in lieu of the cash. Particularly for money-market funds, whose repos are typically done in the tri-party format, this is not a desirable outcome. A money-market fund may therefore demand its cash at the first opportunity that day and fail to renew tri-party repos. The clearing bank could then be exposed during the day to the extent that it had provided credit to the dealer bank in anticipation of "re-winding" the dealer's repo positions at the end of the day, and to the extent that the market value of the dealer's securities is not adequate.

A tri-party clearing bank would normally monitor the intra-day "net free equity" of a dealer counterparty, checking that the

TABLE 3.2
Variation in repo haircuts.

Typical haircut on term securities financing transactions (percent)

	June 2007			June 2009		
	Prime[a]	Non-prime[b]	Unrated[c]	Prime[a]	Non-prime[b]	Unrated[c]
G7 government bonds						
Short-term	0	0	0.5	0.5	1	2
Medium-term	0	0	0.5	1	2	3
U.S. agencies						
Short-term	1	2	3	1	2	3
Medium-term	1	2	3	2	5	7
Pfandbrief	0	0	1	1	2	8
Prime MBS						
AAA-rated	4	6	10	10	20	30–100
AA-rated and A-rated	8	12	25	100	100	100
Asset-backed securities	10	20	20	25	50	100
Structured products (AAA)	10	15	20	100	100	100
Investment grade bonds						
AAA- and AA-rated	1	2	5	8	12	15
A-rated and BBB-rated	4	7	10	10	15	20
High-yield bonds	8	12	20	15	20	40
Equities						
G7 countries	10	12	20	15	20	25
Emerging economies	15	20	35	20	25	40

Notes: [a]Prime counterparty. [b]Non-prime counterparty. [c]Hedge funds and other unrated counterparties.

Source: Committee on the Global Financial System (2010: 2).

total market value of the dealer's cash and securities (including commitments) remains positive, but traditionally allowing "daylight overdraft" cash transfer privileges. This allows dealers to manage more easily the sequencing of settlements of its transactions during the day, as explained by Tuckman (2010). The clearing bank normally maintains the legal right to refuse to process cash payments when the dealer's creditworthiness is of concern. If the dealer fails, the clearing bank could itself be forced to sell repo collateral, or to use the collateral to obtain a secured loan from another bank or from its central bank. Faced with this prospect, a clearing bank might withdraw access to tri-party repo and other clearing services from the dealer, or block the return to the dealer of large amounts of its collateral, further reducing the dealer's financial flexibility.

Thus, a suspicion that a dealer may not meet its repo obligations could be self-fulfilling, for a dealer would be unlikely to be able to continue its daily operations if its ability to finance its securities in the repo market were suddenly to disappear. This exemplifies the importance of the various credit facilities initiated by the New York Federal Reserve Bank in 2008. The Primary Dealer Credit Facility, for example, effectively extended to investment banks a source of financing for securities that had previously been available only to regulated banks through the discount window.

A dealer bank can mitigate the risk of a loss of liquidity through a run by short-term creditors by establishing lines of bank credit, by dedicating a buffer stock of cash and liquid securities for emergency liquidity needs, and by "laddering" the maturities of its liabilities so that only a small fraction of its debt needs to be refinanced within a short period of time.[19] In the face of doubts by its counterparties, a dealer bank that in actuality has sufficient balance-sheet flexibility may have enough time to raise capital and arrange alternative lines of financing, thereby controlling its need to conduct fire sales and allowing it to weather a solvency storm. Major dealer banks have teams of professionals that manage liquidity risk by controlling the distribution of liability maturities and by managing the availability of pools of cash and of noncash collateral that is acceptable to secured creditors.

Dealer banks may have access to secured financing from various types of central-bank backstop financing facilities. The European Central Bank (ECB) provides repo financing to Eurozone banks through regular auctions, by which the ECB accepts a wide range of collateral at moderate haircuts. This repo facility acts as a liquidity backstop. Research by Cassola, Hortacsu, and Kastl (2008) shows that from August 2007, when the range of collateral that was acceptable in the OTC repo market narrowed after a rash of subprime mortgage defaults, Eurozone banks bid significantly more aggressively for financing in ECB repo auctions. The U.S. Federal Reserve has always provided secured financing to regulated banks through its discount window. Discount-window financing, however, is available for a restricted range of high-quality collateral, and its use is believed to stigmatize any banks that are so weak as to need to use it. Dealers that are not regulated financial institutions do not have access to the discount window. During the financial crisis, special credit facilities were established by the U.S. Federal Reserve, allowing even non-bank dealers to arrange financing of a range of assets, or to exchange a range of less liquid assets for treasury securities.[20] Even the use of these facilities, however, seemed to have carried something of a stigma. Valukas (2010) reports, for example, that Lehman was reluctant to use the Primary Dealer Credit Facility (PDCF) for this reason.[21] Almost immediately after the failure of Lehman, the last two large dealers whose parent firms had not been regulated as bank holding companies, Morgan Stanley and Goldman Sachs, became regulated bank holding companies, giving them access to the discount window, among other sources of government support, such as FDIC deposit insurance and loan guarantees. Tucker (2009) describes a range of new secured financing facilities of the Bank of England.

During a solvency crisis the extent to which the regulated bank affiliates of a dealer are financed by traditional insured bank deposits may lessen the need of the parent bank holding company to replace cash that is lost from the exits of repo counterparties and other less stable funding sources. Insured deposits are less likely to run than are many other forms of short-term liabilities. Under Rule 23A of the Federal Reserve Act, however, U.S.-regulated banks may not use deposits to fund their broker-dealer affiliates.

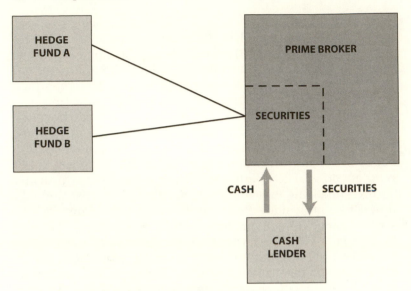

Figure 3.2.   Rehypothecation of prime-brokerage assets.

DISAPPEARANCE OF PRIME-BROKERAGE CLIENTS

For some dealer banks, prime brokerage is an important source of fee revenue. Under normal conditions, dealer banks can also finance themselves in part with the cash and securities that clients leave in their prime-brokerage accounts, as illustrated in figure 3.2.

One says that a customer's assets are "segregated" from those of its prime broker if the assets are held in separate accounts to which the customer has a legally traceable property right and that are distinct from the broker's own accounts. If a customer's assets are not segregated, then the customer merely holds a contractual claim against the broker. As a result, in the event of the broker's bankruptcy, the customer continues to own the securities in a segregated account, but may need to pursue claims against the dealer for any unsegregated assets.

In the United Kingdom, securities and cash in prime-brokerage accounts are not required to be segregated. Customer assets are often commingled with the prime broker's own assets, and thus available to the prime broker for its business purposes, including secured borrowing. Cash in unsegregated

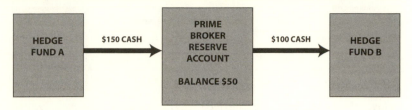

Figure 3.3. A prime broker lends $100 million to Hedge Fund B from funds deposited by Hedge Fund A.

prime-brokerage accounts is, for practical purposes, equivalent to uninsured deposits. Prime brokers operating under U.S. rules may or may not fully segregate their clients' cash, depending on the situation, according to Rule 15c3-2 governing the treatment of "free credit balances," the amount of cash that a client has a right to demand on short notice.[22] Under Rule 15c3-3, however, a U.S.-regulated prime broker must aggregate its clients' free credit balances "in safe areas of the broker-dealer's business related to servicing its customers" or otherwise deposit the funds in a reserve bank account to prevent commingling of customer and firm funds.[23] The ability to aggregate cash associated with clients' free credit balances into a single pool, although separate from the prime broker's own funds, provides flexibility to a prime broker in managing the cash needs of its clients through the ability to use one client's cash balances to meet the immediate cash demands of another.

For example, suppose for simplicity that a dealer has two prime-brokerage clients. It holds cash belonging to Hedge Fund A of $150 million each, and has given a cash loan to Hedge Fund B for $100 million. The excess cash of $50 million must be held in a reserve account, as illustrated in figure 3.3. If Hedge Fund A suddenly withdraws its cash, however, then the prime broker would need to quickly come up with $100 million of cash from new sources in order to finance its loan to Hedge Fund B. Thus, concerns about a dealer's liquidity that leads some customers to switch to another prime broker could exacerbate the dealer's liquidity problems.

Loans by prime brokers to their clients are normally secured by the assets of those clients. For U.S.-regulated prime brokers, the amounts of such margin loans are limited by advance rates that are set according to asset classes. For example, the

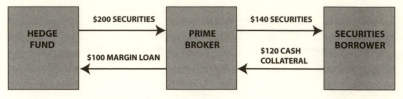

Figure 3.4. In this example, a prime broker borrows $120 million by rehypothecating $140 million of the assets of a client, to whom it lent $100 million, for a net cash financing to the prime broker of $20 million.

maximum amount of cash that can be advanced for equities is 50% of the market value of the equities. Margin loans can be financed by using the client's own assets as collateral for a loan from a third party. Specifically, the prime broker can obtain the cash that it lends a client, as well as additional cash for its own purposes, by rehypothecating the client's securities as collateral on a secured loan from another lender. For each $100 of margin cash, the dealer is permitted to rehypothecate $140 worth of the client's assets, as illustrated in figure 3.4. Under U.S. Rule 15c3-3, however, the prime broker may not obtain more financing based on rehypothecation, in total across all customers, than the aggregate amount of margin loans granted to customers. Rehypothecation of securities received from prime-brokerage clients through London accounts can be a significant source of financing for the prime broker. In the example illustrated in figure 3.4, the prime broker lends its client $100 million and uses its client's assets to secure a loan for itself of $120 million, thereby netting $20 million in cash to finance itself.

When a dealer bank's financial position is weakened, hedge funds may move their prime-brokerage accounts elsewhere. Failure to run, as Lehman's London-based clients learned, could leave a client unable to claim ownership of assets that had not been segregated in the client's account and had been rehypothecated to third parties.[24] In the United States, ironically, a prime broker's cash liquidity problems can be exacerbated by its prime-brokerage business *whether or not* clients run. Under its contract with its prime broker, a hedge fund could continue to demand cash margin loans from the dealer backed by securities that it has left in its prime-brokerage account, but a prime broker whose solvency is known to be questionable may no longer be able to obtain the necessary cash to fund a loan to that customer by using those same securities as collateral for loans from other investors. The dealer's potential repo counterparties and other sources of secured loans may, as explained earlier, find it preferable to lend elsewhere. Thus, the *absence* of a run by prime-brokerage clients could temporarily exacerbate a dealer's liquidity crisis, through an effective expansion of the dealer's need for cash. A dealer could therefore even have an incentive to "fire" a prime-brokerage client in order to avoid providing cash margin financing to the client. On the other hand, as explained earlier, if prime-brokerage clients run, the cash that they pull from their free credit balances is no longer available to meet the cash demands of other clients on short notice, so the prime broker may be forced to use its own cash to meet these demands.

In summary, the exit of prime-brokerage clients can eliminate a valuable source of liquidity to a prime broker. Clients that do not move to another prime broker may, in the face of concerns over their broker's solvency, move some of their securities into custody accounts or otherwise restrict the access of the prime broker to the securities.

Singh and Aitken (2009) calculate from 10Q and 10K reports that between August 2008 and November 2008, the securities that Morgan Stanley had received from its clients that were available for Morgan Stanley to pledge to others declined by 69%, as illustrated in figure 3.5. If, as in the example of figure 3.4, Morgan Stanley had been able to obtain $20 dollars in financing for every $140 dollars of client securities that it was permitted to rehypothecate, then the reduction of approximately $600 billion in repledgeable client assets shown in figure 3.5 would have represented a reduction of over $80 billion in cash financing sources.

For Merrill Lynch and Goldman Sachs, the corresponding declines in repledgeable collateral over this short period spanning the default of Lehman were 51% and 30%, respectively.[25]

The flight of prime-brokerage clients in the face of a dealer bank's financial weakness could also raise concerns among potential providers of emergency capital over the prime broker's long-run profitability. Immediately after the failure of Lehman,

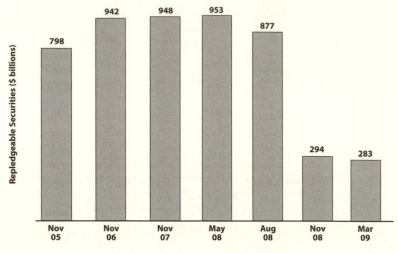

Figure 3.5. Assets pledged to Morgan Stanley that it was permitted to re-
pledge dropped radically after the failure of Lehman (dollars, in billions).
Data: SEC filings collected by Singh and Aitken (2009).

some hedge funds moved away from Morgan Stanley and Goldman Sachs for at least a portion of their prime-brokerage services. In the days immediately following Lehman's default, the
cost in the CDS market of covering $100 million of senior un-
secured Morgan Stanley debt against default losses began to
exceed $10 million per year.

Some analysts believe that hedge funds are likely to diversify
further their sources of prime brokerage, and in the future to
place more of their assets with custodian banks rather than
with traditional prime brokers.[26]

A notable recent innovation to the prime-brokerage segregation model is a three-way custodial contract whose parties are
a hedge fund, a dealer bank (typically the prime broker of the
hedge fund), and a custodian bank.[27] This contractual innovation is designed to protect the dealer from the hedge fund's
failure, without putting the hedge fund's collateral at risk. By
such an arrangement, a portion of the assets that the hedge
fund places in a custodian account are legally assignable to the
dealer, contingent on the failure of the hedge fund to meet its
obligations. In the event that the dealer itself fails, the hedge
fund has immediate access to its assets.

Loss of Clearing and Settlement Privileges

The final step in the collapse of a dealer bank's ability to meet its daily obligations could be a simple refusal by its clearing bank to process transactions that could bring the cash balances in the dealer's clearing account below zero during the course of a business day, *after subtracting* any potential exposures of the clearing bank to the dealer.

In the normal course of business, a clearing bank may decide to extend daylight overdraft privileges to creditworthy clearing customers. For example, the cash required to settle a securities trade on behalf of a dealer client could be wired to the dealer's counterparty (or that counterparty's own clearing bank) before the necessary cash actually appears in the dealer's clearing account on that day, under the premise that the dealer will receive sufficient cash later that day in the course of settling other transactions. Meanwhile, the dealer has securities in its clearing account with a market value that is likely to be more than sufficient to cover any potential shortfall.[28] This daylight overdraft privilege is based in part on the overnight settlement convention of the interbank loan market, by which one has met one's cash settlement obligations for a given day provided that the cash due is sent before the end of the business day. Interest is not typically calculated on the basis of intraday balances, although daylight overdrafts are sometimes assessed a small proportional fee. In the U.S. interbank market, cash payments are settled by FedWire electronic transfer of federal funds from one bank's account with the Federal Reserve to another's. For the purposes of determining the interest earned on federal funds deposits, as well as for meeting reserve requirements, what matters to a clearing bank on a given day is its federal funds balances as of 6:30 p.m. EST. Abate (2009:2) estimated that the intraday peak level of overdrafts occurs at about 10 a.m., and "easily exceeds several hundred billion dollars."

When a dealer's cash liquidity comes into doubt, however, its clearing bank could apply its "right of offset," a contractual right that is normally granted by clearing-account holders, giving the clearing bank the right to offset against the account holder's cash balances its potential exposures to the account holder through other obligations. This gives the clearing bank the right to discontinue making cash payments that would reduce the account holder's cash balance below zero during the day, after accounting for such offsets.[29]

In the context of Lehman's shrinking sources of financing, for instance, Valukas (2010:4:1241–44) reports that Citigroup informed Lehman that Citi believed that it held a right of offset against a $2 billion Lehman deposit, and that Citi "subjected the deposit to a number of internal controls designed to retain the funds at Citi." That this action amounted to an effective loss of liquidity for Lehman is apparent from the fact that "Lehman included the deposit in its reported liquidity pool," and that Lehman disputed the right of Citi to hold Lehman's deposit at Citi. In August, according to Lehman, "JPMorgan reduced Lehman's intraday credit position by $5 billion, requiring [Lehman] to pledge additional collateral for a like amount" (Valukas, 2010:4:1102).[30] As September approached, as reported by Valukas (2010), Lehman was under significant pressure to produce additional collateral to cover the exposures of several of its clearing banks, Citi, HSBC, Bank of America, and, most importantly, J. P. Morgan Chase.[31]

Just before Lehman failed, its principle clearing bank, J. P. Morgan Chase, finally threatened to refuse to process Lehman's instructions to wire cash needed to settle Lehman's trades with its counterparties, by relying on agreements by which J. P. Morgan Chase had the right to offset Lehman's obligations across a range of repo, broker-dealer, and OTC derivatives activities. Valukas (2010:4:1165) reports that on September 11, 2008, J. P. Morgan demanded an additional $5 billion in cash collateral to cover its daylight exposure to Lehman: "Pursuant to the notice, if JPMorgan did not receive this collateral by the opening of business on September 12, 2008, JPMorgan would 'exercise [its] right to decline to extend credit to [Lehman] under the [Clearance] Agreement.'" In light of its right of offset, a clearing bank could freeze some of the assets held by a dealer in its clearing accounts by declaring these assets to be collateral against the dealer's obligations to the clearing bank.[32] Finally, after a frenzied weekend of communications with J. P. Morgan over collateral disagreements, Lehman's holding company was unable to meet its obligations and entered bankruptcy on September 15, 2008.

CHAPTER FOUR

Recapitalizing a Weak Bank

THIS CHAPTER REVIEWS some impediments to the prefailure re-capitalization of a weakened systemically important financial institution, such as a major dealer bank. It also explores two "automatic" recapitalization mechanisms. The first is distress-contingent convertible debt, which consists of claims to interest and principal that automatically convert to shares of equity if and when the financial institution fails to meet a stipulated capital requirement. The second mechanism is a regulation mandating an offer to existing shareholders to purchase new equity at a low price when a financial institution fails to meet a stipulated liquidity or capital requirement. These relatively new approaches overcome some of the adverse incentives for recapitalization.

INCENTIVES AGAINST RECAPITALIZATION

When a financial institution has a low level of capital relative to its assets, there are several impediments to its recapitalization, absent regulation.

The existing equity owners of the financial institution are typically reluctant to issue new equity. The price at which new equity can be successfully issued is likely to be so dilutive as to be against their interests. Despite the potential for new capital to reduce significantly the firm's distress costs, a large amount of the total-firm value added by new equity capital would go toward improving the position of creditors, who would otherwise absorb losses at default. Current shareholders are not interested in donating wealth to debt holders. This roadblock to equity issuance, called debt overhang, was first explained by Myers (1977).

An earlier version of this chapter appears in *Ending Government Bailouts as We Know Them*, Hoover Institution Press, 2010.

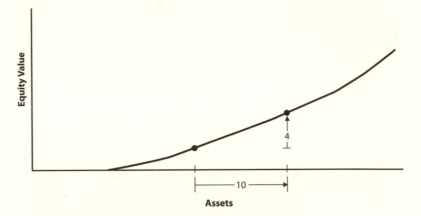

Figure 4.1. Illustration of debt overhang.

Figure 4.1 illustrates the idea of debt overhang. In the example shown, a weak bank could potentially be recapitalized with an increase in assets of $10 billion raised by issuing new equity. This would reduce the bank's financial distress to the extent that the market value of the bank's debt increases by, say, $6 billion. In perfect markets, the total market value of equity and the total market value of debt would increase by the amount of new capital, $10 billion, implying that the total market value of equity has increased by $4 billion. Because the new equity owners must have been given equity worth at least $10 billion (otherwise, they would not have paid $10 billion in cash for their new shares), it follows that the market value of the shares held by the old equity owners must have gone *down* by $6 billion. Thus, in perfect markets, the old equity owners would not allow the issuance of new shares. Reducing the market imperfection associated with distress costs would provide some incentive for a share issuance, but in this case the reduction in distress costs would need to benefit the total market value of equity by at least $6 billion in order to convince the old equity owners of the merits of the new issuance.

Beyond the debt-overhang impediment to raising capital, new shares offered to the market by a weak financial institution may be viewed by potential buyers as "lemons." A potential investor might ask, "Why would I pay $10 a share if the bank is willing to sell shares at that price? The bank knows more than I about the value of the new shares. Thus, if the bank is willing to sell at $10, then the shares could be worth at most $10, and possibly much less." This impediment to a sale is called adverse selection. It often follows, as suggested by Akerlof (1970) as well as Leland and Pyle (1977), that the new shares would need to be sold at such a low price that the existing shareholders would prefer that they were not offered at all.

Raising cash from the sale of assets is also unattractive to equity owners. By lowering the leverage of the financial institution, they would lose the advantage of profiting from any upside return on the assets while retaining the option to default if the return on assets is poor, in which case creditors (or taxpayers) would absorb the default losses. Furthermore, asset sales may themselves suffer from a severe "lemons" discount.

Faced with the prospect of severe bankruptcy costs, the creditors of the weakened financial institution might prefer to reduce voluntarily their contractual claims. For example, by offering to exchange each dollar of debt principal for a package of new debt and equity claims worth a market value of 75 cents, they would come out ahead if this avoids a bankruptcy in which they would recover only 50 cents in market value. Frequently, however, the creditors of a firm that is headed for bankruptcy are unable to coordinate such an out-of-court restructuring. If all but one of them were to agree to this, for example, then the last has an incentive to hold out, given the likelihood that the restructuring would save the firm from default, leaving the hold-out creditor with a full payment of his original claim. Perhaps the remaining creditors would be willing to go ahead anyway, bailing out one or a few small hold-out creditors, but rarely would the remaining creditors avoid a defection in their own ranks. This situation is sometimes called a "prisoners dilemma." Even though creditors would be better off, as a group, to commit to a restructuring of their claims, it is unusual in practice to obtain a sufficient number of individual consents.

Bankruptcy is normally an effective mechanism for breaking through the recapitalization gridlock just described. A distressed firm can emerge from bankruptcy with a new and less risky capital structure. More broadly, as has been shown in a range of theoretical settings by Innes (1990), Hart and Moore

(1998), and DeMarzo and Duffie (1999), a conventional capital structure consisting of pure equity and pure debt, with a bankruptcy-style boundary condition, is an efficient contractual approach for raising capital and for allocating a firm's cash flows and control rights. This theoretical foundation, however, does not consider the economy-wide costs of systemic risk, which go beyond the costs and benefits that matter to creditors and equity holders.

For the failure resolution of systemically important financial institutions such as large dealer banks, alternatives include special bankruptcy procedures, as proposed by Jackson (2010), and government-coordinated receiverships or conservatorships, as explained by Kroener (2010). These approaches consider the costs and benefits to the taxpayer and the general economy. The objective of these proposals is to improve the balance between firm-level efficiency and economy-wide costs.

The remainder of this chapter is devoted to complementary prefailure mechanisms for restructuring distressed financial institutions.

DISTRESS-CONTINGENT CONVERTIBLE DEBT

As originally envisioned by Flannery (2005), distress-contingent convertible bondholders receive equity shares in lieu of future claims to interest and principal if and when the issuer fails to meet certain capital requirements, as illustrated in figure 4.2.

Various designs have been proposed for the distress trigger and for the conversion ratio, which is the number of shares of equity to be received in exchange for each dollar of bond principal.[1] I will discuss these later. There are also various proposals for the degree to which such debt issues would contribute to meeting a financial institution's regulatory capital requirement. It is also an open issue whether the issuance of distress-contingent convertible bonds would be a regulatory requirement or an optional method of meeting capital requirements, in which case regulators would need to specify the quantitative formula by which distress-contingent convertible debt, equity, preferred shares, and other instruments would be weighted in measuring a bank's regulatory capital. If the issuance of distress-contingent convertible bonds is not required

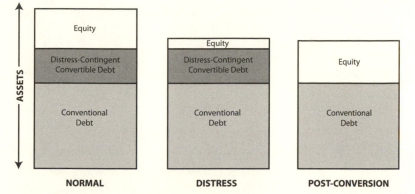

Figure 4.2. Distress-contingent convertible debt converts to equity when a bank's leverage hits a distress trigger level.

by regulation, an incentive to issue these contingent securities could be based on an adjustment to tax codes that allows their preconversion interest payments to be deductible from income for tax purposes, just as for ordinary corporate debt. Historical precursors to the notion of distress-contingent securities, such as income bonds and stock cancelation schemes, are reviewed by Skeel (1993).

In November 2009, Lloyds Bank announced the issuance of £7.5 billion of such bonds, called "Enhanced Capital Notes" or "CoCos," with conversion to common equity if the bank's Tier 1 capital ratio were to fall to 5 percent. The Royal Bank of Scotland was said to be planning a similar issuance. These announcements were part of a general recapitalization of these two banks that includes new equity rights issues and involves a participating investment by the United Kingdom. The president of the New York Federal Reserve, William Dudley, as well as the chairman of the Federal Reserve System, Ben Bernanke, have spoken in favor of the general concept of distress-contingent convertible debt for systemically important financial institutions.[2] The governor of the Bank of England, Mervyn King, although more skeptical, has said that these instruments are "worth a try." Regulatory support for contingent capital was included among the financial reforms proposed under the version of the Restoring American Financial Stability Bill being considered by Congress in 2010.

If the trigger for automatic conversion is an accounting capital ratio, such as the Tier 1 capital trigger used in the design of the Lloyds Bank issuance, there should be some concern over the failure of accounting measures to capture the true financial condition of the bank. For example, Citibank, a systemically important financial institution that did receive a significant government bailout during the recent financial crisis, had a Tier 1 capital ratio that never fell below 7 percent during the course of the financial crisis and was measured[3] at 11.8 percent at roughly its weakest moment in December 2008, when the stock market capitalization of Citibank's holding company fell to around $20 billion, or about 1 percent of its total accounting assets. Because of the limited-liability treatment of equity and because of significant prevailing uncertainty over the true valuation of Citibank's assets, this stock market valuation suggests that Citibank's assets probably had a market value well below its debt principal in late 2008. Nevertheless, any reasonable tripwire based on Tier 1 capital would probably not have been tripped.

If restricted to accounting measures of capitalization, perhaps a more effective trigger could be based on the ratio of tangible common equity (TCE) to tangible assets, a measure that excludes preferred shares and intangible assets such as goodwill and tax shields from net-operating-loss carry-forwards, all of which are relatively useless assets during a solvency crisis. At the end 2008, Citibank had tangible common equity of only $31 billion,[4] for a TCE ratio of about 1.5 percent, effectively signaling that Citibank was substantially less well capitalized than most of its peers. (Among large banks, only the Bank of New York–Mellon had a similarly low tangible common equity capital ratio.) The "S-Cap" stress tests, by which the U.S. government measured shortfalls in the capitalization of large banks in the spring of 2009, were based instead on accounting common equity (which includes goodwill). Even tangible common equity reacts slowly to market conditions, given the typical lag in marking down bad loans for accounting purposes.

Nevertheless, a trigger based on tangible common equity seems worthy of serious consideration. If, instead, the envisioned debt is converted to equity when the market value of equity falls to a sufficiently low level, then, depending on the conversion price and the number of new equity shares created, short-sellers may be tempted to attack the issuer's stock in order to trigger the conversion and profit from the resulting dilution or the reduction in the market value of equity shares associated with a reduced value of the option to default. Short-sellers might further increase their profits by acquiring the convertible debt in advance of attacking the stock, so as to obtain new shares cheaply through conversion. Even in the absence of such an attack, merely a rational assumption by some shareholders that sales of shares by other shareholders might trigger a conversion could indeed lead many shareholders to fulfill this prophecy, through the resulting short-term impact of sudden sales on share prices. Markets need not be so efficient that bargain-hunting buyers of shares would react quickly enough to offset the downward price impact caused by sellers.

Such a self-generating decline in share prices, sometimes called a "death spiral," could be mitigated by a trigger that is based instead on a trailing average share price, for example, the average closing price of the shares over the preceding twenty business days. In that case, any adverse price impact on a given day would receive a weight of 1/20 toward the price used in the conversion trigger.

Yet another approach is to use a trigger based on the bank's credit default swap (CDS) rate.[5]

Flannery (2009) explains that the incentive for a speculative attack is lessened or eliminated by a sufficiently high contractual conversion price P, according to which each dollar of principal of debt is converted to $1/P$ shares. Flannery notes that if the conversion price is higher than the trigger price of equity (that market price for shares at which conversion is contractually triggered), then conversion is effectively antidilutive, raising the price of shares. This leaves open the question of how to set the trigger price and the conversion price so that, despite any antidilutive effect of conversion, the original equity holders have a strong incentive to keep the financial institution well capitalized.

The presence of distress-contingent convertible debt in the capital structure of a dealer bank is unlikely to stop a liquidity crisis once it begins. Short-term creditors, over-the-counter (OTC) derivatives counterparties, and prime-brokerage clients who anticipate the potential failure of the bank are unlikely to be dissuaded from a run merely by the fact that the future principal and interest claims of the bonds have been converted to equity. This conversion does nothing for the immediate cash position of the bank. Once a rush for the exits begins, it is rational that it would continue in a self-fulfilling manner. The trigger that converts the debt to equity should be set so as to eliminate the debt claims before a liquidity crisis is likely to begin, and hopefully with a sufficiently strong impact on the balance sheet to forestall a self-fulfilling presumption of a liquidity crisis.

One could also contract so that the cash proceeds of a contingent-convertible debt issue are escrowed, say, in a trust, and become available to the issuer in cash only when the debt is converted to equity.[6] This improves the cash position of the bank at a time of distress, albeit at the cost to the bank of idling the cash raised until that time.

Mandatory Rights Offerings of Equity

Distressed financial institutions, among other firms, sometimes offer rights to existing shareholders to purchase new shares at a price that is well below the current market price. Given the effects of debt overhang and adverse selection, an offering price near the current market price is unlikely to be exercised by many shareholders. When offered at a sufficiently low price, however, many existing shareholders would subscribe, given that a failure to do so would result in a costly dilution of their share claims and an effective transfer of wealth to those who do subscribe. Any shareholders without the cash necessary to take up the offer would do best by selling their shares before the expiration of the offer to those who do have the cash. (In some cases, the rights themselves can be sold.) Thus, a mandatory rights offering at a sufficiently low price is likely to be well subscribed, so long as the issuer indeed has some value left in its business for long-run equity investors.

During the financial crisis of 2007–2009, nine major European banks collectively raised over $120 billion dollars using mandatory rights offerings, usually at deep discounts.[7] The lack of rights offerings by major U.S. banks during the financial crisis is not easily explained, but it could be related to the relatively dispersed ownership of these banks, which raises the risk of under subscription of the offering.

A rights offering at a low price largely finesses the adverse-selection problem that I described earlier. In effect, the buyers and the sellers of the new shares are the same investors. Nevertheless, because of debt overhang, the existing shareholders may in many cases prefer not to conduct such a mandatory rights offering. Thus, due to the social costs of systemic risk, it may be appropriate to introduce a regulation that forces an automatic rights offering as soon as a financial institution hits specified tripwires in its measured financial condition.[8] If the short-term creditors, clients, and other counterparties of a financial institution know that a rights offering of sufficient size will occur at stipulated liquidity triggers, they may view a liquidity crisis to be sufficiently unlikely that they would not have the incentive to start one with a run.

Even under existing U.S. regulations, banks are required to issue new shares, or otherwise raise new regulatory capital, when they do not meet stipulated capital-adequacy standards. In practice, however, most banks that had failed have not been forced to raise new capital under these regulations. Presumably, the triggers are not sufficiently well designed, or regulators have used excessive forbearance.

As opposed to the conversion of debt to equity, a mandatory rights offering provides new cash that may reduce the risk of a liquidity crisis. Indeed, the presence of a regulation mandating a rights offering when the capital position of a financial institution deteriorates may forestall the self-fulfilling prophecy of a run by creditors and others who have the discretion to drain cash from the weakened institution. Because of the time lag between the offering and the cash settlement of the new share purchases, however, even a mandatory rights offering is unlikely to stop a run in progress. The triggers must be set so that the new shares are sold before the cash is likely to be needed. Thus, as opposed to the case of distress-contingent convertible debt, there should be a bias toward triggers that are based on the cash liquidity of the financial institution, as opposed to overall balance-sheet solvency.

are in principle sufficient to cover its liabilities in an orderly liquidation of its balance sheet.

The forced sale of illiquid assets in order to generate cash can lead to losses. In addition to the price discount caused by a forced sale to a limited set of immediately available buyers, the liquidation values of assets can be further reduced by adverse selection. As explained in chapter 4, the potential buyer, knowing less than the seller about the future asset cash flows, should offer a price so low that the buyer's informational disadvantage is not an issue. This same principle limits the bank's ability to raise cash by issuing debt or equity. As a mitigating factor, if the seller is known to be experiencing a liquidity crisis, the probability of adverse selection, at a given offering price, is lowered. In a financial crisis, however, those potential bidders who would normally be in the best position to make use of the assets are themselves likely to be in a cash-constrained position, and may themselves wish to raise capital or to sell the same types of assets.

An alternative to raising cash from the outright sale of assets is to use assets as collateral for secured borrowing. As a bank's solvency prospects dim, however, the opportunity to obtain even secured financing is reduced. When a dealer experiences a liquidity crisis, it can be given discriminatory terms for haircuts and collateral pricing. The room for maneuvering through a liquidity crisis diminishes as the inventory of unpledged high-quality collateral, such as treasury securities, is reduced. Eventually, the repo market can cease to provide the financing necessary to keep assets on the dealer bank's balance sheet. By this point, even a fire sale of assets is unlikely to stave off failure. Bankruptcy can follow quickly, as it did for Lehman Brothers.

During the financial crisis, the U.S. Federal Reserve System and the Bank of England provided a range of new secured lending facilities as backstop sources of financing to large dealer banks, as explained by Tucker (2009). The European Central Bank's conventional repo operations continued to provide financing to banks for a wide range of assets.

Going forward, large dealer banks should be held to significantly higher liquidity standards. The Basel Committee on Banking Supervision (2009) has suggested a minimum "liquidity coverage ratio" of 100%, meaning that for every potential dollar of cash outflows within thirty days, a bank would need to demonstrate to regulators that it has at least one dollar in unencumbered highly liquid assets. The proposed definition of this liquidity coverage ratio does not, however, consider the dependence of a dealer bank on short-term financing opportunities presented by its access to the assets of its clients and derivatives counterparties. As explained in chapter 3, when hedge funds "run" from their prime broker, the assets they had "parked" with the prime broker may no longer be available to the prime broker as a source of financing. Likewise, when OTC derivatives counterparties run away from a weakened dealer bank, they withdraw the collateral they had left with the dealer—collateral that the dealer is likely to have used as a source of financing. The reliance of a dealer bank on these unstable sources of short-term financing is a source of liquidity risk that should be considered in the design of minimum regulatory liquidity ratios.

To meet its minimum liquidity needs, a dealer bank should be required to demonstrate that it can roll over its short-term borrowing, even if haircuts on secured loans and repurchase agreements are raised dramatically. To that end, repurchase agreements collateralized by riskier assets whose haircuts could change adversely during a financial crisis should not be relied upon as a source of short-term financing. Further, unsecured loans should have dispersed maturities, so that there is never a large fraction of debt coming due within a short period of time.

UTILITIES FOR TRI-PARTY REPO CLEARING

As I have explained, short-term repurchase agreements can represent an unstable source of dealer financing. In the face of concerns over a dealer's solvency, the cash lender can simply invest the cash with a more reliable repo counterparty. In the case of tri-party repurchase agreements, the discretion of the clearing bank to continue offering clearing services is a particular concern. If the clearing bank has a credit exposure to the dealer, for example, through a daylight overdraft (as explained in chapter 3) or other lines of business, then the risk to the clearing bank itself is a system-wide concern. If the clearing bank exercises its discretion to discontinue providing credit to a dealer during the day, or to discontinue clearing the dealer's trades, or to make significant demands for additional collateral from the dealer, then the dealer may be forced to shut down.

Bernanke (2008) has pointed to the potential benefits of a tri-party repo "utility," which would have less discretion in rolling over a dealer's repo positions and fewer conflicting incentives. Operational controls might be more cleanly monitored.[1] The separation of tri-party repo clearing from other clearing-bank functions would, however, reduce a dealer's cash-management flexibility, and thus lower its potential leverage under normal operating conditions. This is an efficiency cost that is to be compared with the gain in financial stability that can be achieved by separating tri-party repo from other clearing-bank services.

Abate (2009) mentions the potential for Federal Reserve insurance of tri-party repo transactions. Another approach under discussion is an "emergency bank," which would be financed by repo market participants and which could manage the orderly unwinds of repo positions of weakened dealers. The emergency bank would have access to discount-window financing from the central bank, and would insulate systemically critical clearing banks from losses in the course of the unwinding process. While these alternative approaches have some advantages during a crisis, they increase moral hazard by increasing the incentives of market participants to take risks in the normal course of business, given the "bailout" backstop.

Regardless of the tri-party format, strong standards should be established for the documentation of trades, for margin, for caps on daylight overdrafts, and for the daily substitution of collateral that takes place over the course of term repos.[2] Improvements in transparency should include the public disclosure of the amounts of collateral of each type that are placed in tri-party repos, as well as the average haircuts that are applied to each class of collateral. Based on this disclosure, market participants would be in a better position to judge the potential for an unstable market condition. Tuckman (2010) recommends new risk-based capital requirements that reflect the intraday risks faced by clearing banks.

Rules limiting the speed with which repo haircuts are adjusted may mitigate the adverse feedback caused when increases in haircuts generate price reductions.

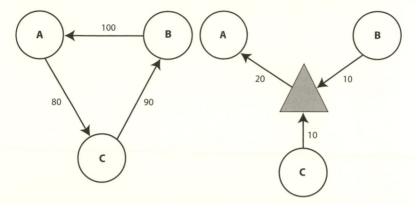

Figure 5.1. The reduction in counterparty exposure achieved with multilateral netting.

CENTRAL CLEARING OF OTC DERIVATIVES

The threat to a dealer posed by the flight of its OTC derivatives counterparties can be lowered by central clearing. Sufficiently extensive clearing can also reduce the total exposure to the dealer, through the multilateral netting of positive against negative exposures that occurs with clearing. For example, as illustrated in figure 5.1, suppose that, before considering the effect of collateral, Dealer A is exposed by $100 million to Dealer B, while Dealer B is exposed to Dealer C for $90 million, and Dealer C is exposed to Dealer A for $80 million. In addition to insulating A, B, and C from each other's default risk, central clearing significantly reduces the exposures. Once all three dealers have cleared their positions, the central clearing counterparty (CCP), represented in figure 5.1 by a triangle, is able to net the receivables and payables of each dealer. For example, Dealer A is now exposed to a maximum loss of $20 million, before considering collateral. In addition to lowering the counterparty risks facing each dealer, thereby lowering the need for expensive collateral posting, these reductions in exposures to counterparty risk also lower systemic risk.

Reductions in exposure risk through central clearing require, however, that clearing is sufficiently centralized, as explained by Duffie and Zhu (2009). This is illustrated in figure 5.2, which assumes that Dealer C clears all of its derivatives through a

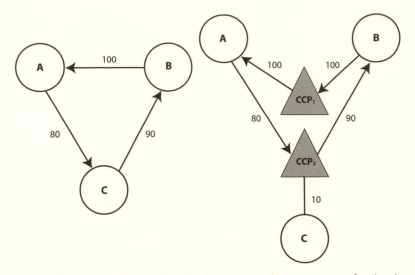

Figure 5.2. A significant reduction in counterparty exposure reduction is lost with multiple CCPs.

different CCP than that used in trades between *A* and *B*. With the two CCPs, counterparty exposures remain high, and there is an unnecessarily high demand for collateral, which, aside from its cost, may discourage dealers and other market participants from clearing their derivatives.

Obviously, the effectiveness of central clearing depends heavily on the financial strength and risk management of central clearing counterparties. Duffie, Li, and Lubke (2010) describe the importance of proper supervision, capitalization, collateral standards, and risk management of CCPs. (These issues are reviewed briefly in the appendix.) Once a CCP has cleared a significant amount of derivatives, it is itself a source of systemic risk, which may justify a need for implicit government backing. Like a tri-party repo utility, however, a CCP has limited discretion. The moral hazard faced by a CCP that is "too big to fail," while a concern, is unlike that arising from the discretion, scope, and flexibility of risk-taking by a major dealer that is too big to fail.

Currently, the majority of OTC derivatives positions are not cleared. There are currently no plans for clearing significant quantities of OTC derivatives that are based on equities, commodities, and foreign exchange. Although large quantities of interest rate swaps are cleared, the majority are not.

CONTINGENT CAPITAL

Dealers will need to pin down a substantial amount of additional capital to run their businesses in the face of significant progress on the central clearing of derivatives, tri-party repo utilities, and rigorous liquidity coverage ratios. Some degree of efficiency in the capital structure of a large financial institution might, however, be recovered through contingent capital. One form of contingent capital, explained in chapter 4, consists of debt-like claims to interest and principal that, contingent on stipulated distress triggers, convert to equity. Significant amounts of well-designed contingent capital will mitigate moral hazard, costly and systemically disruptive asset fire sales, and—after conversion—debt overhang. Another promising form of contingent capital is a regulation stipulating triggers for a mandatory equity rights offering, to be made at a deep discount to the current equity price. By this mechanism, whenever the specified capital or liquidity ratios of a systemically important financial institution drop below a specified minimum, the financial institution would be required to make such a rights offering immediately, as needed to regain financial stability. Such rights offerings have advantages over contingent convertible debt because (1) they bring immediate cash to the distressed financial institution, and (2) they recruit new capital into the financial sector, which is especially valuable during a financial crisis. An equity rights offering may also offer some additional flexibility in creating an incentive for a financial institution to remain well capitalized.

IMPROVED FAILURE RESOLUTION

It seems inevitable, despite pending improvements in regulation, best practices, and market infrastructure, that major financial institutions will fail from time to time. Among other steps, Richard Herring (2010) and the Squam Lake Working

Group on Financial Regulation (2010) recommend clearly formulated wind-down plans, sometimes known as "living wills," that effectively terminate or assign financial contracts without creating significant unnecessary frictional losses through fire-sales and counterparty or creditor distress. As Herring (2010) explains, this is especially challenging and important in an international setting, in which resolution authorities or courts in each sovereign jurisdiction can apply significantly different approaches and incentives.

Mechanisms for the resolution of failing large dealer banks at the level of their holding companies are not yet effective. AIG, a type of financial institution that is not within the scope of this study, is a prime example of a large financial institution that was judged too big to fail, and was extremely costly for the U.S. government to stabilize with only those regulatory tools available at the time. As explained by U.S. Federal Reserve Chairman Ben Bernanke, U.S. regulators did not believe that they had the necessary regulatory tools to resolve Lehman Brothers, other than by allowing it to enter bankruptcy.

Proposals for the improved resolution of systemically important financial institutions by an adjustment to bankruptcy law are proposed by Jackson (2010) and Jackson and Skeel (2010). An alternative, the use of government-coordinated receiverships or conservatorships, is explained by Kroener (2010) and is pending enactment in the Restoring American Financial Stability Bill of 2010.

It is not clear yet, however, whether either of the proposed resolution mechanisms will effectively treat dealer banks with large amounts of overnight repo financing and with significant uncleared OTC derivatives portfolios, which present special difficulties, as explained by Bliss (2003) and Edwards and Morrison (2005).

Some proposals for the failure resolution of large financial institutions could have the unintended consequences of increasing the incentive for creditors and other counterparties to "run." For example, the discretion held by a resolution authority to initiate a resolution process could raise uncertainty among creditors regarding the potential timing of any such initiative, and generate doubt over the treatment of their claims against the failing institution. Faced with such uncertainty, a run by creditors might be accelerated. In the case of OTC derivatives and repurchase agreements, a run of this type could be accelerated if counterparties and creditors that have the ability to run on short notice would be harmed in the event of a resolution process that would stay their contracts for any significant period of time, or even if their contracts are not stayed but are terminated under a threat of significant loss. The bankruptcy approach, if well designed, is likely to offer less discretion, and thus be more predictable in its consequences for counterparties and creditors. This would lower the risk of a run.

Central Clearing of Derivatives

THIS APPENDIX, which draws directly from Duffie, Li, and Lubke (2010), is an introduction to the central clearing of derivatives.

Counterparty credit risk can often be reduced by "clearing," which means obtaining the effect of a guarantee by a central counterparty (CCP), sometimes called a clearing house. The CCP stands between the two original counterparties, acting as the seller to the original buyer, and as the buyer to the original seller. In order to be financially resilient, a CCP relies on a range of controls and methods, including stringent membership access, a robust collateral regime, clear default management procedures, and significant financial resources that back its performance.

Because its long and short positions are automatically offsetting, a CCP has no losses or gains on a derivatives contract so long as the original counterparties to the trade continue to perform. The CCP is, however, exposed to counterparty credit risk from each of its participants. Because of this risk, and because of the systemic importance of CCPs, regulators and CCPs should demand strict acceptance criteria from market participants that wish to obtain the right to clear their trades with CCPs by becoming clearing members. Clearing members must also provide liquid margin assets that can be used to offset losses to the CCP in the event that the member fails to perform on its cleared derivatives positions. A CCP collects two types of collateral from each member: "initial margin," provided when a trade is cleared, and "variation margin," which is exchanged between the CCP and the clearing member on a daily basis. On any day, the variation margin payment is the estimated change in the market value of the derivatives position from the previous day. The determination of initial and variation margins is discussed in more detail later in this appendix.

Beyond demonstrating its financial strength and providing margin, each CCP member must also contribute capital to a pooled CCP guarantee fund. The guarantee fund is an additional layer of resources, after initial margin, to cover losses stemming from the failure of a member to perform on a cleared derivative. For example, suppose that Counterparty X fails, and as a result "owes" the CCP $100 million, reflecting the cost to the CCP of unwinding its derivatives positions with X. Suppose that X had posted $80 million in margin with the CCP. The CCP would first apply this margin toward the unwinding costs. The remaining $20 million necessary to unwind the failed derivatives positions with X would be taken from the other resources of the CCP, which include the pooled guarantee fund. The procedures followed and the forms of financial backing available to the CCP depend on the particular rules of the CCP. An example is provided at the end of this appendix.

The amount of initial margin posted with a CCP is based on an analysis, sometimes complex, of the risks posed to the CCP by the type of the derivative in question, as well as by the size of the position. The initial margin for each type of derivatives contract is based in part on the volatility of changes in the market value of that type of derivative, bearing in mind that there is a delay between the times at which a variation margin payment is determined and the time by which the derivatives contract could be liquidated in an orderly manner by the CCP, should the clearing member fail to provide the variation margin. The initial margin should exceed, in most extreme scenarios, the change in market value of the derivatives position over this time window. For example, the initial margin for a credit default swap is generally greater than that for an interest rate swap of the same notional size because of the potential of sudden changes in the credit quality of the borrowers referenced in most credit default swaps. The determination of initial margins should also consider the potential for adverse changes in the liquidity of the financial instrument during the unwind period. For example, the difference between the bid and offer prices for some types of derivatives could suddenly increase during a period of financial stress.

The process of daily variation margin determination requires daily estimates of the fair-market prices of each of the types of derivative cleared by the CCP. Because of the costs of analyzing risks and of setting up pricing methods for each type of derivative cleared, as well as other fixed setup costs, it is not cost effective to clear types of derivatives that are thinly traded or complex. In addition to the high cost of handling thinly traded or complex derivatives, a CCP may face a sudden need to unwind positions held with a failed clearing member. If forced to liquidate positions on thinly traded derivatives on short notice, the CCP could have difficulty avoiding the losses caused by fire-sale discounts.

For a moderately sized position in an actively traded derivative, it may take only a day or two for the CCP to unwind its position without incurring a severe additional fire-sale loss. For a large position in a less actively traded type of derivative, the CCP could take much longer to unwind its position in order to avoid causing itself a large additional fire-sale loss. Thus, the appropriate amount of initial margin for each type of derivative reflects both the daily volatility of the market value of the derivative as well as the number of days that is likely to be needed for an orderly unwind of the position. This is one of the key reasons that central clearing is not appropriate for thinly traded types of derivatives.

The initial margin required on a derivatives position could naturally be set equal to an estimate of the daily volatility of the market value of the position, multiplied by two days plus the number of days required to unwind the position in an orderly manner, and further multiplied by a safety factor. The addition of two days is appropriate because the variation margin payment requested on a given day would typically be determined based on the closing price of the previous day and might be received (or found to be missing) on the following day. If the first sign of trouble is the failure of a counterparty to make a margin payment, it could take up to two days from the last price determination for a CCP to realize that it must begin to unwind the counterparty's position.

We give a hypothetical example of the determination of the initial margin for a given derivatives position.

Suppose a CCP has historically cleared an average daily notional amount of $100 million of a particular type of derivative. An orderly unwind for this type of derivative is estimated to require the liquidation on each day of no more than 20% of the daily average clearing volume, which is $20 million in this case. A counterparty wishes to clear a trade with a notional position size of $60 million. The counterparty is assumed to have no prior positions in this type of derivative. At an orderly unwind rate of $20 million per day, the $60 million notional position would require a three-day safe-unwind period. Allowing for two initial days to begin an unwind, the initial margin should therefore cover the change in market value that could occur in an extreme but plausible scenario over a total period of five days. The daily volatility of each $1 million notional of this type of derivative is estimated to be $2,000. Thus, a position of $60 million represents an estimated daily volatility of $120,000. Because the daily volatility represents a typical daily price change, and because the margin should cover a stress scenario, we suppose that the CCP or its regulator has mandated a safety factor for this type of derivative of 3.5. The initial margin for a position size of $60 million would then be five days worth of volatility multiplied by $120,000 of position volatility per day, and further multiplied by a stress factor of 3.5, which is $2.1 million in total. This calculation ignores the "diversification" benefit associated with a lack of perfect correlation of price changes over successive days.

If a CCP is successful in clearing a large quantity of derivatives trades, the CCP is itself a systemically important financial institution. The failure of a CCP could suddenly expose many major market participants to losses. Any such failure, moreover, is likely to have been triggered by the failure of one or more large clearing members, and therefore to occur during a period of extreme market fragility. Thus, while robust operational and financial controls are paramount in reducing the likelihood of a CCP failure, a CCP must also have methods in place for quickly recapitalizing, or for quickly unwinding its derivatives positions with minimal impact on counterparty risks and on the underlying markets. Regulators should ensure that a CCP's risk-management design and financial resources are robust enough to allow the CCP to withstand extreme but plausible loss scenarios. Recent experience has shown that current international standards, which call only for protection against the failure of the single largest participant in "extreme but plausible" market conditions, are insufficient. Regulatory standards should ensure that CCPs remain resilient to a broader set of risks, including multiple participant failures, sudden fire sales of financial resources, and rapid reductions in market liquidity.

Extreme but plausible loss scenarios should encompass, at a minimum, the largest historical observed price movements in that market. The corresponding sizing of the guarantee fund and other resources should be reassessed by the CCP and its regulators on a regular basis.

In the event that a clearing participant is unable to meet its contractual obligations, its CCP typically has several layers of financial resources upon which to draw. The primary objective of the CCP in such a scenario is to be able to continue to meet its contractual obligations as a counterparty to each of its non-defaulting participants. In so doing, it prevents the propagation of systemic risk. Depending on its design, a typical CCP may have several layers of protection against the cost of unwinding the derivatives positions of any defaulting member. In the order in which they are drawn upon, these might be among the following: (1) the initial margin posted by the failing participant, (2) the contribution of that participant to the CCP guarantee fund, (3) a "first-loss" pool of capital of the CCP, (4) the portion of the pooled guarantee fund provided by the non-defaulting members, and (5) a contractual claim to additional contributions by CCP participants, contingent on losses to the guarantee fund. In practice, the designs of CCPs vary, and may include these and additional financial resources for handling default management.

We can illustrate with an example of how the various financial resources of a CCP are engaged in a scenario with multiple failures of clearing members. Consider the scenario depicted in figure A.1, from Duffie, Li, and Lubke (2010). Here, perhaps in the course of a severe and sudden financial crisis, several members of a CCP fail in sequence. In the scenario shown in figure A.1, Participant A is the first to default. For example, on a given day, A has failed to make its required variation margin payment. Under the rules of this particular CCP, the derivatives positions of the failed participant are auctioned to the surviving participants. Each derivatives position of A is auctioned separately. For each position, that member offering to assume A's position at the lowest cost to the CCP wins. The total of the winning bids across all of A's positions is the cost to the CCP of unwinding A's positions (before considering administrative costs). This total cost is shown in the figure as the height of the

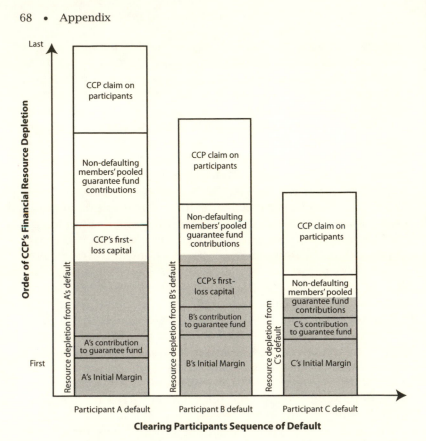

Figure A.1. The waterfall of resources available to a CCP. Source: Duffie, Li, and Lubke (2010).

shaded portion of the "Participant *A*" column. As shown, this unwind cost exceeds the initial margin that *A* had provided to the CCP, despite the intention that the initial margin should cover the unwind cost in most extreme scenarios. Indeed, this illustrated scenario is so extreme that the unwind cost exceeds the sum of the initial margin and the contribution of *A* to the guarantee fund. The remainder of the unwind cost is funded out of the "first-loss" capital held by the CCP for this eventuality. In practice, the derivatives positions may be auctioned in packages, rather than individually.

After *A* defaults, in this example, Participant *B* defaults. The unwind cost for *B* is covered by the initial margin that had been posted by B, then the contribution by B to the guarantee fund, and then the remainder of the first-loss capital of the CCP, which has already been partly depleted by the default of A. Participant B's default takes place before the CCP has replenished its first-loss capital. The cost of unwinding B's derivatives positions is so large in this scenario that even some of the guarantee fund was required to cover it. Finally, Participant C fails. By this point, the first-loss capital of the CCP had been fully exhausted by the failures of A and B. There has been insufficient time for the CCP to replenish its first-loss capital and guarantee fund. As shown in the figure, the cost of unwinding C's positions also requires some use of the now-reduced pooled guarantee fund. Ultimately, the CCP has sufficient resources to unwind its derivatives positions with A, B, and C, while continuing to perform on its derivatives positions with non-defaulting participants. The CCP then restores its guarantee fund and first-loss capital.

Notes

NOTES TO PREFACE
1. See Tucker (2010).

NOTES TO CHAPTER ONE
INTRODUCTION
1. Bliss and Kaufman (2006) review the distinctions between bank and non-bank failure resolution.
2. See Horwitz (2009).

NOTES TO CHAPTER TWO
WHAT IS A DEALER BANK?
1. The primary dealers that are not part of financial groups represented in table 2.1 are Cantor Fitzgerald and Jeffries & Company (which are both interdealer brokers), Daiwa Securities America, Inc., Mizuho Securities USA, Inc., Nomura Securities International, and the Royal Bank of Canada. The dealers shown in table 2.1 that are not also primary dealers in U.S. government securities are Commerzbank AG, Société Générale, and Wells Fargo.
2. For potential synergies between commercial and investment banking, see Kanatas and Qi (2003).
3. For a case example of lapses in risk oversight, see UBS (2008), the "Shareholder Report on UBS's Writedowns," especially chapter 5, "Risk Management and Control Activities."
4. See the White House press release January 21, 2010, "President Obama Calls for New Restrictions on Size and Scope of Financial Institutions to Rein in Excesses and Protect Taxpayers," at www.whitehouse.gov/the-press-office/president-obama-calls-new-restrictions-size-and-scope-financial-institutions-rein-e.
5. See ISDA, MFA, and SIFMA (2009).
6. See http://www.dtcc.com/products/derivserv/.
7. Statistics on the use of compression trades are provided by Duffie, Li, and Lubke (2010).
8. See Hintz, Montgomery, and Curotto (2009).
9. See Barr (2007b). As it turned out, this and another similarly bolstered internal hedge fund failed in the following month. See Barr (2007a).

10. See Goldman Sachs (2007).

11. CNBC (2008) reported, "The Citi-managed fund, known as Falcon, was brought onto the bank's books, which will increase the bank's assets and liabilities by about $10 billion."

12. See Goldstein (2007).

13. See Moyer (2007).

NOTES TO CHAPTER THREE
FAILURE MECHANISMS

1. See International Swaps and Derivatives Association (2004).

2. Yavorsky (2008) reports that "[a]ny perceived appearance, or actual presence, of significant problems faced by a firm, may lead to a sudden spike in CDS novation requests, as counterparties seek to reduce their exposure to the firm. In addition to the operational burden of processing such requests, a high number of novation requests can become a liquidity-draining event as existing counterparties, with which the firm has a net receivable position, move their trades away and withdraw cash collateral in the process. Similarly, when counterparties, with which the firm has a net payable position, assign their trades to new counterparties, the firm may be required to meet higher collateral requirements, including initial margin. While the firm is under no contractual obligation to consent to novation, it may feel pressured to do so in order to satisfy its customers, as well as to preserve the appearance that it has ample liquidity resources (any appearance to the contrary can be immediately devastating to its ability to access other confidence-sensitive sources of liquidity). Such a sudden 'cash call,' if unplanned for, particularly if combined with other difficulties experienced by the firm, can have very negative self-fulfilling consequences. This risk was highlighted by (and likely played a role in) the near collapse of Bear Stearns, which had become an active participant in the CDS market." Leising (2009) reported that "Dealers such as JPMorgan, Goldman Sachs Group Inc. and UBS AG are working with ICE Trust on a framework in which client funds would be granted protections against counterparty default, such as segregated collateral accounts. The lack of segregated accounts led to losses for funds that posted excess collateral with Lehman Brothers last year after the securities firm filed for bankruptcy protection. This 'structural flaw' in the over-the-counter market was evident in the weeks leading to the collapse of Lehman Brothers and Bear Stearns last year, Lubke [Theo Lubke, of the New York Federal Reserve] said. 'We saw a tremendous outflow of liquidity from each

bank,' he said. 'Their buy-side counterparties didn't want to lose their initial margin if there was a bankruptcy proceeding.'"

3. Because the net collateral that is due to be paid to, or received from, a counterparty is calculated daily, based on the positions at the end of the previous day, and because any such cash flows would normally be sent on the day after they are determined, there could be a delay of two days or more between the date on which OTC derivatives positions are eliminated and the date on which the associated collateral cash is actually returned.

4. See New York Federal Reserve Bank (2009).

5. See page 7 of ISDA, MFA, and SIFMA (2009).

6. Such thresholds are sometimes stated in terms of the short-term credit rating, and they stipulate additional collateral upon downgrade below "prime," which is a rating of P1 by Moodys or A1 by Standard and Poors.

7. The legal procedures for this process that are to be followed in Lehman's bankruptcy are documented in Lehman Bankruptcy Docket (2008a) and Lehman Bankruptcy Docket (2008b). Lehman-creditors.com provides related dockets. For an overview of the treatment of Lehman's derivatives in bankruptcy, see Summe (2010). Dealers work largely under the terms of ISDA's standard 2002 master swap agreement. The 2002 standard agreement is substantially more flexible regarding the method of determining the replacement value of terminated positions than is the 1992 agreement, which bases default settlement claims on third-party quotations. Some OTC derivatives counterparties continue to operate under the 1992 agreement.

8. See http://www.occ.treas.gov/deriv/deriv.htm.

9. See Wall, Tallman, and Abken (1996).

10. Yavorsky (2008:9) writes, "During the weekend of September 13–14, as the possibility of Lehman's default began to loom large, major CDS counterparties, including dealers, hedge funds and other buy-side firms, arranged an emergency 'Lehman Risk Reduction Trading Session.' The purpose of the session was to determine a list of derivative trades (including credit, equity, rates, FX and commodity derivatives) to which Lehman was a counterparty, and then close them out by entering into offsetting replacement trades with one another to 'bypass' Lehman. In accordance with a protocol drafted by ISDA, the replacement trades became contingent on Lehman Brothers actually filing for bankruptcy. According to a number of market participants, the close-out session resulted in the replacement of only a relatively limited amount of all the outstanding trades. This reflected, in part, the difficulty of determining and agreeing on the new prices of the trades as participants naturally

expected significant price volatility (rising credit spreads, falling equity markets, etc.) the following Monday. It also reflected the sheer operational difficulty of replacing a substantial volume of trades involving multiple counterparties within a limited amount of time. As a result, many of the trades had to be replaced in subsequent days and weeks, with the price of CDS protection, in particular, having by then moved appreciably higher."

11. This trigger is known as "credit event upon merger," although it does not require a merger.

12. See Bank for International Settlements (2007), Bliss and Steigerwald (2006), Duffie and Zhu (2009), Hills et al. (1999), and Ledrut and Upper (2007).

13. At the default of Lehman, Global Association of Central Counterparties (2009) describes the performance of central clearing counterparties in processing the closeout or novation of some of Lehman's derivatives positions.

14. See "Weekly Release of Primary Dealer Positions, Transactions, and Financing as of June 2009," on the website of the New York Federal Reserve Bank. I am grateful to J. A. Aitken for directing me to these data.

15. Valukas (2010) reports that Lehman's leverage was substantially larger than publicly disclosed because of inappropriate accounting of "Repo 105" transactions, which were effectively added to assets and liabilities, but were not recorded as such.

16. Valukas (2010:1092–93) writes that "Craig Delany, a managing director at JPMorgan's Investment Bank, however, stated that, in triparty repos, typically investors look to the counterparty (i.e., broker-dealer) first and the collateral second when setting haircuts. In other words, a haircut may not be sufficient for an investor if it has serious concerns about the viability of its counterparty."

17. In the United States, money market funds, typically operating under Rule 2a-7 of the Securities and Exchange Commission, have restrictions on the types of assets they are permitted to hold and would be required to sell immediately many of the forms of collateral that they could receive in the event that a repo counterparty fails to perform. For text of this rule, see the *Securities Lawyers Deskbook* published by the University of Cincinnati College of Law at http://www.law.uc.edu/CCL/InvCoRls/rule2a-7.html.

18. Fisher (2008) states, "I would also suggest that the prevalence of repo-based financing helps explain the abruptness and persistence with which the de-levering has been translated into illiquidity and sharp asset price declines." Ewerhart and Tapking (2008) and Hordahl and King (2008) review the behavior of repo markets during the financial crisis. Gorton (2010) provides estimates of the haircuts

applied to various classes of securities before and during the financial crisis. In July 2007, corporate bonds and structured credit products of many types, both investment grade and non-investment grade, had haircuts of 2% or less. From the second quarter of 2008, many classes of these securities had haircuts in excess of 20%, while a number of classes of securities are shown by Gorton's source to have had no financing in the repo market.

19. See Financial Services Authority (2009) and the section on liquidity risk management in the February 22, 2010 10K (for year-end 2009) of Goldman Sachs.

20. These facilities include the the Single-Tranche OMO Program, the Term Discount Window Program, the Term Auction Facility, the transitional credit extensions announced on September 21, 2008, the Primary Dealer Credit Facility, the Term Securities Lending Facility, the Commercial Paper Funding Facility, and the Term Asset-Backed Securities Loan Facility.

21. Valukas (2010:4:1396) reports that "[p]aradoxically, while the PDCF was created to mitigate the liquidity flight caused by the loss of confidence in an investment bank, use of the PDCF was seen both by Lehman, and possibly by the broader market, as an event that could trigger a loss of confidence. A report by Lehman Brothers Capital Markets Prime Services captured a common critique of the facility: 'PDCF borrowing has a considerable stigma in spite of the Fed's efforts to cloak access and guarantee anonymity. Instead, primary dealers view the PDCF as a last resort and will exhaust all other financing sources before pledging collateral here. For this reason, borrowing at this program has evaporated since the [Bear Stearns] merger closed."

22. Rule 15c3-2 of the Securities and Exchange Act of 1934, "Customers' Free Credit Balances," states that "No broker or dealer shall use any funds arising out of any free credit balance carried for the account of any customer in connection with the operation of the business of such broker or dealer unless such broker or dealer has established adequate procedures pursuant to which each customer for whom a free credit balance is carried will be given or sent, together with or as a part of the customer's statement of account, whenever sent but not less frequently than once every three months, a written statement informing such customer of the amount due to the customer by such broker or dealer on the date of such statement, and containing a written notice that (a) such funds are not segregated and may be used in the operation of the business of such broker or dealer, and (b) such funds are payable on the demand of the customer: Provided, however, that this section shall not apply to a broker or dealer which is also a banking institution supervised

and examined by State or Federal authority having supervision over banks. For the purpose of this section the term customer shall mean every person other than a broker or dealer."

23. See Securities and Exchange Commission (2002).

24. See, for example, Farrell (2008), Mackintosh (2008), and Singh and Aitken (2009). Aragon and Strahan (2009) estimate the degree to which those hedge funds whose prime broker was Lehman Brothers were harmed by the bankruptcy of Lehman.

25. Singh and Aitken (2009) emphasize that the significant recent general reductions in the availability of pledgeable collateral securities may lead to a systemic shortage of collateral, which could lead to liquidity problems.

26. I refer to King et al. (2008) and Hintz, Montgomery, and Curotto (2009).

27. See Devasabai (2009).

28. Valukas (2010:4:1093), for example, writes, "As triparty-repo agent to broker-dealers, JPMorgan was effectively their intraday triparty lender. When JPMorgan paid cash to the triparty investors in the morning and received collateral into broker-dealer accounts (which secured its cash advance), it bore a similar risk for the duration of the business day that triparty lenders bore overnight. If a broker-dealer such as LBI [Lehman Brothers International] defaulted during the day, JPMorgan would have to sell the securities it was holding as collateral to recoup its morning cash advance."

29. Valukas (2010:4:1093) notes that "JPMorgan used a measurement for triparty and all other clearing exposure known as Net Free Equity (NFE). In its simplest form, NFE was the market value of Lehman securities pledged to JPMorgan plus any unsecured credit line JPMorgan extended to Lehman minus cash advanced by JPMorgan to Lehman. An NFE value greater than zero indicated that Lehman had not depleted its available credit with JPMorgan. The NFE methodology also enabled JPMorgan to monitor its exposure position at all times during the trading day and thereby evaluate collateral substitutions by Lehman that might produce undesired credit exposures. If a trade would put Lehman's NFE below zero, the trade would not be permitted. Through February 2008, JPMorgan gave full value to the securities pledged by Lehman in the NFE calculation and did not require a haircut for its effective intraday triparty lending. Consequently, through February 2008, JPMorgan did not require that Lehman post the margin required by investors overnight to JPMorgan during the day."

30. Valukas explains the fact that Lehman itself marked the value of the collateral, which was often in the form of collateralized debt

obligations whose true valuations were dubious, at least in the eyes of J. P. Morgan.

31. Lehman also presented some intraday exposure to the Bank of New York Mellon over Lehman's program for borrowing with commercial paper and medium-term notes.

32. Dey and Fortson (2008) write (see, also, Teather (2008) and Craig and Sidel (2008)) that "[t]he giant American bank [J. P. Morgan Chase] is alleged to have frozen $17 billion (£9.6 billion) of cash and securities belonging to Lehman on the Friday night before its failure." Sender (2009) reports, "In addition to serving as its clearing agent, J. P. Morgan was also Lehman's biggest counterparty on billions of dollars of derivatives trades. In such transactions, each side tots up its net exposure every night, demanding additional collateral when the amounts owed exceed a certain threshold. If Lehman defaulted, according to the agreements, the value at which these trades were automatically closed out was determined by J. P. Morgan. On August 26, J. P. Morgan reworked its existing credit agreements with Lehman so that the parent guaranteed the obligations of the broker-dealer and also provided collateral to secure that guarantee.... Then, on September 4, J. P. Morgan was briefed on Lehman's upcoming earnings results and was told it expected to report a $4bn loss, according to people familiar with the matter. Five days later, J. P. Morgan signed another agreement with Lehman in which the Lehman parent's guarantee covered not just its failing broker-dealer but all Lehman entities and covering all transactions, including the large book of derivatives trades.... The creditors' committee now alleges that J. P. Morgan had collected about $17 bn in collateral from Lehman in the first two weeks of September 2008. A filing on behalf of unsecured creditors states that as of the Friday before the bankruptcy petition, the Lehman holding company had 'at least $17bn in excess assets in the form of cash and securities' that were held by J. P. Morgan and subsequently frozen by J. P. Morgan. 'JPMC's refusal to make those assets available to [Lehman] and its subsidiaries in the days leading up to the bankruptcy filing may have contributed to Lehman's liquidity constraints,' the filing claims."

NOTES TO CHAPTER FOUR
RECAPITALIZING A WEAK BANK

1. See Raviv (2004), HM Treasury (2009), and Portes (2009).
2. See Bernanke (2009b) and Dudley (2009).

3. Citibank's Tier 1 capital ratio was 7.1 percent in the fourth quarter of 2007. See, for example, http://seekingalpha.com/article/115374-citigroup-inc-q4-2008-earnings-call-transcript?page=1.

4. See www.citibank.com/citi/fin/data/090807a.pdf.

5. I am grateful to Viral Acharya for this suggestion. Stewart Myers has commented that if the contingent capital is presumed by CDS investors to be effective, then the CDS rate would not be especially sensitive to declining capital, suggesting a problem for this approach.

6. This possibility was suggested to me by Joe Grundfest.

7. See Duffie (2010) for details.

8. I am grateful to Peter DeMarzo for suggesting this approach, which is a subject of ongoing research by the two of us.

NOTES TO CHAPTER FIVE
IMPROVING REGULATIONS AND MARKET INFRASTRUCTURE

1. See also Bernanke (2009a), Tuckman (2010), and Payments Risk Committee (2009).

2. See Bank for International Settlements (2009b), Payments Risk Committee (2009), and Tuckman (2010).

Bibliography

Abate, Joseph. "Money Markets: Tri-party Repo Concerns." Barclays Capital, Research, U.S. Economics & Rates, Strategy, March 12, 2009.

Akerlof, George. "The Market for 'Lemons': Quality Uncertainty and the Market Mechanism." *Quarterly Journal of Economics* 84, no. 3 (1970): 488–500.

Aragon, George O., and Philip E. Strahan. "Hedge Funds as Liquidity Providers: Evidence from the Lehman Bankruptcy." Working paper, Boston College, August 26, 2009.

Bank for International Settlements. "New Developments in Clearing and Settlement Arrangements for OTC Derivatives." Technical report, Bank for International Settlements (BIS), Basel, March 2007. Available at www.bis.org/publ/cpss77.htm.

———. a. "OTC Derivatives Market Activity in the Second Half of 2008." BIS Monetary and Economic Department, Basel, May 2009. Available at www.bis.org/publ/otc_hy0905.pdf.

———. b. "The Role of Valuation and Leverage in Procyclicality." BIS, April 2009. Available at www.bis.org/publ/cgfs34.pdf.

Barr, Alistair. a. "Bear Stearns' Credit Hedge Funds Almost Wiped Out: Leveraged Fund Worth Nothing; 'Very Little Value' Left in Larger Fund, Letter Says." *MarketWatch*, July 18, 2007. Available at www.marketwatch.com/story/bear-credit-hedge-funds-almost-wiped-out-sources-say.

———. b. "Bear to Lend $3.2 Bln to One of Its Hedge Funds—But Bank Doesn't Lend Money to Other, More Leveraged, Hedge Fund." *MarketWatch*, June 22, 2007. Available at www.marketwatch.com/story/bear-to-lend-up-to-32-bln-to-troubled-hedge-fund-it-runs.

Basel Committee on Banking Supervision. "International Framework for Liquidity Risk Measurement, Standards and Monitoring." Technical Report, Bank for International Settlements, December 2009. Available at www.bis.org/publ/bcbs165.pdf.

Bernanke, Ben. "Reducing Systemic Risk." Speech presented at the Federal Reserve Bank of Kansas City's Annual Economic Symposium, Jackson Hole, Wyoming, August 22, 2008.

———. a. "Financial Reform to Address Systemic Risk." Speech presented to the Council on Foreign Relations, March 10, 2009.

Bernanke, Ben. b. "Financial Regulation and Supervision after the Crisis: The Role of the Federal Reserve." Remarks given at the Federal Reserve Bank of Boston 54th Economic Conference, October 13, 2009.

Bliss, Robert R. "Resolving Large Complex Financial Organizations." Pp. 3–31 in George G. Kaufman, ed., *Market Discipline in Banking: Theory and Evidence*, vol. 15. Amsterdam: Elsevier Press, 2003.

Bliss, Robert R., and George G. Kaufman. "U.S. Corporate and Bank Insolvency Regimes: An Economic Comparison and Evaluation." Working Paper WP-06-01, Federal Reserve Bank of Chicago, 2006.

Bliss, Robert R., and Robert Steigerwald. "Derivatives Clearing and Settlement: A Comparison of Central Counterparties and Alternative Structures." *Economic Perspectives* 30, no. 4 (2006): 22–29.

Boot, Arnoud, Todd Milbourn, and Anjun Thakor. "Megamergers and Expanded Scope: Theories of Bank Size and Activity Diversity." *Journal of Banking and Finance* 23, no. 2 (1999): 195–214.

Brunnermeier, Markus K., and Lasse Heje Pedersen. "Market Liquidity and Funding Liquidity." *Review of Financial Studies* 22, no. 6 (2008): 2201–38.

Bulow, Jeremy, and Paul Klemperer. "Reorganising the Banks: Focus on the Liabilities, Not the Assets." Web comment, March 21, 2009. Available at www.voxeu.org/index.php?q=node/3320.

Burroughs, Bryan. "Bringing Down Bear Stearns." *Vanity Fair*, August 2008, pp. 106–11.

Cassola, Nuno, Ali Hortacsu, and Jakub Kastl. "Effects of the Subprime Market Crisis on the Primary Market for Liquidity." Working paper, Stanford University, Economics Department, November 2008.

CNBC. "Citigroup to Bail Out Internal Hedge Fund." CNBC.com, February 23, 2008. Available at www.cnbc.com/id/23308202.

Cohan, William D. *House of Cards*. New York: Doubleday, 2009.

Committee on the Global Financial System. "The Role of Margin Requirements and Haircuts in Procyclicality." CGFS Paper Number 36, Bank for International Settlements, Basel, March 2010.

Craig, Susanne, and Robin Sidel. "J.P. Morgan Made Dual Cash Demands." *Wall Street Journal*, October 8, 2008. Available at http://online.wsj.com/article/SB122342716816213665.html.

Culp, Christopher L. "Contingent Capital Versus Contingent Reverse Convertibles for Banks and Insurance Companies." *Journal of Applied Corporate Finance* 20, no 4 (2009): 19–27.

DeMarzo, Peter, and Darrell Duffie. "A Liquidity-Based Model of Security Design." *Econometrica* 67, no. 1 (1999): 65–99.

Devasabai, Kris. "A New Model." *International Custody & Fund Administration*, January 22, 2009. Available at http://icfamagazine. com/public/showPage.html?page=icfa_display_feature&temp PageId=836072.

Dey, Iain, and Danny Fortson. "J. P. Morgan 'Brought Down' Lehman Brothers." *London Times*, Sunday Edition, October 5, 2008.

Diamond, Douglas W., and Philip H. Dybvig. "Bank Runs, Deposit Insurance, and Liquidity." *Journal of Political Economy* 91, no. 3 (1983): 401–19.

Dudley, William. "Some Lessons from the Crisis." Remarks made at the Institute of International Banks Membership Luncheon, New York, October 13, 2009.

Duffie, Darrell. "A Contractual Approach to Resructuring Financial Institutions." Pp. 109–24 in Kenneth Scott and John Taylor, eds., *Ending Government Bailouts as We Know Them.* Stanford: Hoover Press, 2010.

Duffie, Darrell, Ada Li, and Theo Lubke. "Policy Perspectives on OTC Derivatives Market Infrastructure." Technical Report 424, Federal Reserve Bank of New York, January 2010.

Duffie, Darrell, and Haoxiang Zhu. "Do Central Clearing Counterparties Reduce Counterparty Risk?" Working paper, Stanford University, Graduate School of Business, March 2009. Available at www.stanford.edu/~duffie/DuffieZhu.pdf.

Edwards, Franklin, and Edward R. Morrison. "Derivatives and the Bankruptcy Code: Why the Special Treatment?" *Yale Journal on Regulation* 22, no. 1 (2005): 91–122.

Ewerhart, Christian, and Jens Tapking. "Repo Markets, Counterparty Risk, and the 2007/2008 Liquidity Crisis." Working Paper 909, European Central Bank, Frankfurt, 2008.

Farrell, Sean. "Hedge Funds with Billions Tied Up at Lehman Face Months of Uncertainty." *The Independent*, October 6, 2008. Available at www.independent.co.uk/news/business/news/hedge-funds-with-billions-tied-up-at-lehman-face-months-of-uncertainty-9525 86.html.

Financial Services Authority. "Strengthening Liquidity Standards." Technical report, Financial Services Authority, London, October 2009. Available at www.fsa.gov.uk/pubs/policy/ps09_16.pdf.

Fisher, Peter. "Comments on Franklin Allen and Elena Carletti 'The Role of Liquidity in Financial Crises'." Jackson Hole Conference, Wyoming, August 2008. Available at www.kc.frb.org/publicat/sympos/2008/fisher.09.01.08.pdf.

Flannery, Mark J. "No Pain, No Gain? Effecting Market Discipline via Reverse Convertible Debentures." Pp. 171–96 in Hal S. Scott, ed., *Capital Adequacy Beyond Basel: Banking, Securities, and Insurance.* Oxford: Oxford University Press, 2005.

Flannery, Mark J. "Market-Valued Triggers Will Work for Contingent Capital Instruments." Solicited Submission to U.S. Treasury Working Group on Bank Capital, 2009.

Geanakoplos, John. "Liquidity, Default, and Crashes, Endogenous Contracts in General Equilibrium." Pp. 170–205 in M. Dewatripont, L. P. Hansen, and S. J. Turnovsky, eds., *Advances in Economics and Econometrics: Theory and Applications, Eighth World Conference, Volume II,* Econometric Society Monographs. Cambridge: Cambridge University Press, 2003.

Geithner, Timothy. "Reducing Systemic Risk in a Dynamic Financial System." Remarks made at the Economic Club of New York, June 9, 2008. Available at www.bis.org/review/r080612b.pdf.

Global Association of Central Counterparties. "Central Counterparty Default Management and the Collapse of Lehman Brothers." Technical report, CCP12, The Global Association of Central Counterparties, London, 2009.

Goldman Sachs and Company. "Goldman Sachs and Various Investors Including C.V. Starr & Co., Inc., Perry Capital LLC and Eli Broad Invest $3 Billion in Global Equity Opportunities Fund." Goldman Sachs press release, August 13, 2007. Available at www2.goldmansachs.com/our-firm/press/press-releases/archived/2007/2007-08-13.html.

Goldstein, Steve. "HSBC to Provide $35 Billion in Funding to SIVs—Citigroup Reportedly Under Pressure to Move Securities onto its Balance Sheet." *MarketWatch,* November 27, 2007. Available at www.marketwatch.com/story/hsbc-to-provide-35-billion-in-funds-to-structured-vehicles.

Gorton, Gary. *Slapped in the Face by the Invisible Hand: The Panic of 2007.* New York: Oxford University Press, 2010.

Hart, Oliver, and John Moore. "Default and Renegotiation: A Dynamic Model of Debt." *Quarterly Journal of Economics* 113, no. 1 (1998): 1–41.

Herring, Richard. "Wind-down Plans as an Alternative to Bailouts: The Cross Broder Challenges." Pp. 125–62 in Kenneth Scott and John Taylor, eds., *Ending Government Bailouts as we Know Them.* Stanford: Hoover Press, 2010.

Hills, Bob, David Rule, Sarah Parkinson, and Chris Young. "Central Counterparty Clearing Houses and Financial Stability." *Financial Stability Review,* Bank of England, 6, no. 2 (1999): 122–34.

Hintz, Brad, Luke Montgomery, and Vincent Curotto. "U.S. Securities Industry: Prime Brokerage, A Rapidly Evolving Industry." Bernstein Research, March 13, 2009.

HM Treasury. "Risk, Reward and Responsibility: The Financial Sector and Society." Technical report, HM Treasury, December 2009. Available at www.hm-treasury.gov.uk/d/fin_finsectorandsociety. pdf.

Hordahl, Peter, and Michael R. King. "Developments in Repo Markets During the Financial Turmoil." *BIS Quarterly Review*, December 2008, pp. 37–52. Available at www.bis.org/publ/qtrpdf/ r_qt0812e.pdf.

Horwitz, Jeff. "Wachovia's End." *American Banker*, October 13, 2009. Available at http://www.americanbanker.com/news/wachovias_ end-1002613-1.html.

Innes, Robert. "Limited Liability and Incentive Contracting with Ex-Ante Choices." *Journal of Economic Theory* 52, no. 1 (1990): 45–67.

International Swaps and Derivatives Association (ISDA). "User's Guide to the 2004 ISDA Novation Definitions." ISDA technical document, New York, 2004.

——. "ISDA Margin Survey 2009." ISDA technical document, New York, 2009.

——. "The Bankruptcy Code Swap Safe Harbor Overview." ISDA, New York, January 2010.

ISDA, MFA, and SIFMA. "Independent Amounts." Technical report, International Swaps and Derivatives Association, Managed Funds Association, and Securities Industry and Financial Markets Association, October 2009.

Jackson, Thomas H. "Chapter 11F: A Proposal for the Use of Bankruptcy to Resolve Financial Institutions." Pp. 217–52 in Kenneth Scott and John Taylor, eds., *Ending Government Bailouts as We Know Them*. Stanford: Hoover Press, 2010.

Jackson, Thomas H., and David A. Skeel. "Bankruptcy, Banks, and Non-Bank Financial Institutions." Draft prepared for Wharton Financial Institutions Center Workshop, "Cross-Border Issues in Resolving Systemically Important Financial Institutions," February 8, 2010.

Jensen, Michael, and William Meckling. "Theory of the Firm: Managerial Behavior, Agency Costs, and Ownership Structure." *Journal of Financial Economics* 3, no. 4 (1976): 305–60.

Kanatas, George, and Jianping Qi. "Integration of Lending and Underwriting: Implications of Scope Economies." *Journal of Finance* 58, no. 3 (2003): 1167–91.

Kelly, Kate. "Fear, Rumors Touched Off Fatal Run on Bear Stearns." *Wall Street Journal*, May 28, 2008. Available at http://s.wsj.net/article/SB121193290927324603.html.

King, Matt. "Are the Brokers Broken?" Technical report, Citi, European Quantitative Credit Strategy and Analysis, September 2008.

King, Matt, Michael Hampden-Turner, Peter Goves, and Hans Lorenzen. "Where Should Hedge Funds Keep Their Cash?" Citi, European Quantitative Credit Strategy and Analysis, October 2008.

Krimminger, Michael. "The Evolution of U.S. Insolvency Law for Financial Market Contracts." Federal Deposit Insurance Corporation, June 13, 2006.

Kroener, William. "Expanding FDIC-Style Resolution Authority." Pp. 179–88 in Kenneth Scott and John Taylor, eds., *Ending Government Bailouts as We Know Them*. Stanford: Hoover Press, 2010.

Ledrut, Elisabeth, and Christian Upper. "Changing Post-Trading Arrangements for OTC Derivatives." *BIS Quarterly Review* (December 2007): 83–95.

Lehman Bankruptcy Docket. a. "Notice of Debtors' Motion for an Order Pursuant to Sections 105 and 365 of the Bankruptcy Code to Establish Procedures for the Settlement or Assumption and Assignment of Prepetition Derivative Contracts Fed Seeks End to Wall Street Lock on OTC Derivatives." Docket Number 1498, November 13, 2008. U.S. Bankruptcy Court for the Southern District of New York (http://www.nysb.uscourts.gov).

——. b. "Order Pursuant to Sections 105 and 365 of the Bankruptcy Code to Establish Procedures for the Settlement or Assumption and Assignment of Prepetition Derivative Contracts." Docket Number 2257, December 16, 2008.

Leising, Matthew. "Fed Seeks End to Wall Street Lock on OTC Derivatives." Bloomberg.com, May 6, 2009. Available at www.bloomberg.com/apps/news?pid=20601087&sid=adyRr4PP035U.

Leland, Hayne, and David Pyle. "Informational Asymmetries, Financial Structure, and Financial Intermediation." *Journal of Finance* 32, no. 2 (1977): 371–87.

Macey, Jonathan. "Are Bad Banks the Solution to a Banking Crisis?" Unpublished paper, Cornell University, SNS Occasional Paper Number 82, 1999. Available at http://ideas.repec.org/a/eee/jfinec/v54y1999i2p133-163.html.

Mackintosh, James. "Lehman Collapse Puts Prime Broker Model in Question." *Financial Times*, September 24, 2008. Available at www.ft.com/cms/s/0/442f0b24-8a71-11dd-a76a-0000779fd18c.html.

Moyer, Liz. "Citigroup Goes It Alone to Rescue SIVs." *Forbes*, December 13, 2007. Available at www.forbes.com/2007/12/13/citi-siv-bailout-markets-equity-cx_lm_1213markets47.html.

Myers, Stewart. "The Capital Structure Puzzle." *Journal of Finance* 39, no. 4 (1977): 575–592.

New York Federal Reserve Bank. "Report to the Supervisors of the Major OTC Derivatives Dealers on the Proposals of Centralized CDS Clearing Solutions for the Segregation and Portability of Customer CDS Positions and Related Margin." New York Federal Reserve, June 30, 2009.

Office of the Comptroller of the Currency. "OCC's Quarterly Report on Bank Trading and Derivatives Activities: Second Quarter 2009." Technical report, US Department of the Treasury, Washingon, D.C., second quarter, 2009.

Payments Risk Committee. "Task Force on Tri-Party Repo Infrastructure Progess Report." New York, December 22, 2009.

Portes, Jonathan. "Risk, Reward and Responsibility: The Financial Sector and Society." Technical report, VOX, December 2009. Available at www.voxeu.org/index.php?q=node/4417.

Raviv, Alon. "Bank Stability and Market Discipline: Debt-for-Equity Swap versus Subordinated Notes." Technical report, Brandeis University, August 13, 2004.

Securities and Exchange Commission. "Rule 15c3-3: Reserve Requirements for Margin Related to Security Futures Products." 17 CFR Parts 200 and 240 [Release No. 34-50295; File No. S7-34-02] RIN 3235-AI61, 2002.

Sender, Henny. "Lehman Creditors in Fight to Recover Collateral." *Financial Times*, June 21, 2009. Available at www.ft.com/cms/s/0/909ba63c-5e99-11de-91ad-00144feabdc0.html.

Singh, Manmohan, and James Aitken. "Deleveraging after Lehman—Evidence from Reduced Rehypothecation." Unpublished. Working Paper WP/09, International Monetary Fund, 2009.

Skeel, David A. "Markets, Courts, and the Brave New World of Bankruptcy Theory." *Wisconsin Law Review* 2 (1993): 465–521.

Squam Lake Working Group on Financial Regulation. *The Squam Lake Report: Fixing the Financial System.* Princeton, Princeton University Press, 2010.

Summe, Kimberly. "Lessons Learned from the Lehman Bankruptcy." Pp. 59–105 in Kenneth Scott and John Taylor, eds., *Ending Government Bailouts as We Know Them.* Stanford: Hoover Press, 2010.

Teather, David. "Banking Crisis: Lehman Brothers: J. P. Morgan Accused over Bank's Downfall." *The Guardian*, October 6, 2008. Available at http://www.guardian.co.uk/business/2008/oct/06/jpmorgan.lehmanbrothers.

Tucker, Paul. "The Repertoire of Official Sector Interventions in the Financial System: Last Resort Lending, Market-Making, and Capital." Speech delivered to the Bank of Japan 2009 International Conference on Financial System and Monetary Policy: Implementation, Bank of Japan, Tokyo, May 27–28, 2009.

———. "Shadow Banking, Capital Markets and Financial Stability." Speech delivered at BGC Partners Seminar, London, January 21, 2010. Available at www.bankofengland.co.uk/publications/speeches/2010/speech420.pdf.

Tuckman, Bruce. "Systemic Risk and the Tri-Party Repo Clearing Banks." Center For Financial Stability, New York, February 2010.

UBS. "Shareholder Report on UBS's Writedowns." UBS, Zurich, April 18, 2008.

Valukas, Anton. "Report of Anton R. Valukas, Examiner." Vol. 4, In re Lehman Brothers Holdings Inc., Debtors, March 2010.

Wall, Larry D., Ellis W. Tallman, and Peter A. Abken. "The Impact of a Dealer's Failure on OTC Derivatives Market Liquidity during Volatile Periods." Working paper 96-6, Federal Reserve Bank of Atlanta, Georgia, 1996.

Williamson, Christine. "Hedge Fund Ranking Reveals Nasty Scars from Financial Crisis." *Pensions and Investments*, March 8, 2010.

Yavorsky, Alexander. "Credit Default Swaps: Market, Systemic, and Individual Firm Risks in Practice." Moody's Finance and Securities, Investor Report, Special Comment, Moody's Investor Services, October 2008.

Index

Note: numbers in italic indicate references to illustrations